Now Is The Time!

Kingdom Minded

Bridgette Ann

WestBow
PRESS

A DIVISION OF THOMAS NELSON

WestBow Press books may be ordered through booksellers or by contacting:

WestBow Press
A Division of Thomas Nelson
1663 Liberty Drive
Bloomington, IN 47403
www.westbowpress.com
1-(866) 928-1240

Because of the dynamic nature of the Internet, any web addresses or links contained in this book may have changed since publication and may no longer be valid. The views expressed in this work are solely those of the author and do not necessarily reflect the views of the publisher, and the publisher hereby disclaims any responsibility for them.

Any people depicted in stock imagery provided by Thinkstock are models, and such images are being used for illustrative purposes only.

Certain stock imagery © Thinkstock.

ISBN: 978-1-4497-1357-7 (sc)
ISBN: 978-1-4497-1358-4 (e)

Library of Congress Control Number: 2011923705

Printed in the United States of America

WestBow Press rev. date:6/27/2011

Dedication

This book NOW IS THE TIME: KINGDOM MINDED is dedicated to every **saved** **believer** and **all souls** that will be **saved** for the "kingdom of GOD" through the "blood" and resurrection power of JESUS CHRIST our LORD and SAVIOR.

To all new believers go and share the good news of your salvation. Then allow the Lord to plant you with a body (church) of believers where the whole gospel of JESUS CHRIST is being preached and taught. Become a disciple of CHRIST.

Acknowledgements

This work about God's "kingdom" is never accomplished without pain, persistence, spiritual warfare, and solitude. This work grew out of my passion in sharing and evangelizing the "gospel" of Jesus Christ. The passion for millions, billions of souls to be saved for God's "kingdom". The strength and power of the Holy Spirit which resides in me allowed this great work to come to pass. I praise and thank God for the awesome character and nature He has shown me through the power that resides in me as a warrior for Christ, to push me forward in developing this project and revealing it to the world.

I thank God for being a part of Faithful Central Bible Church where Bishop Kenneth C. Ulmer is my Pastor and how the Holy Spirit has allowed him to pour in my Spirit through teaching the Word of God. Thank you Bishop Ulmer.

Dr. Robin J. Grant of "In His Love International Ministry" thanks to God for using you as a vessel to help advance His "kingdom" here on earth. Your love and support of my dreams and visions while walking with me has been a blessing. Thank you!

Thank you God (Daddy) for Reverend Dorcas McReynolds of "Dorcas International Ministries". Reverend Dorcas you are truly an authentic Woman of God through your love, encouragement, and support. Iron sharpens Iron! Spirits knitted together by God.

Thanks to my family, and the few prayer "warriors" God has allowed in my life who has given me encouragement.

I praise and thank God (Daddy) for the three beautiful gifts, Shelley, Shane, and Ugochi, He has blessed me with. Your love and support for what God has chosen and called me to do in advancing His "kingdom" truly have blessed my heart as your mother.

I acknowledge and give God all the honor and glory in using Shelley in this "kingdom assignment" in which the Holy Spirit gave her the creative ideas for the book cover. Thank you for your discernment, wisdom, patience, faithful work and other multi- gifts.

Finally, I thank God (Daddy) for using me as one of His vessels in trusting me to bring forth the Word of God through this work that will save and deliver many by our Lord and Savior Jesus Christ. Glory Be to God in Jesus Name. Amen.

Contents

PREFACE

This book was birth through the power and strength of the Holy Spirit which I was driven to write because of my passion for "souls to be saved" and to share with all believers and non-believers the "urgency" about the "Kingdom of God". This book was written because "Now Is the Time to be Kingdom Minded and to focus more than ever before on the principles and precepts of the "kingdom" that Jesus lived, taught, preached and walked throughout the earth realm. To bring all Christian believers to their true identity, which is the image of God, the "kingdom in you".

To all Christian believers saved and followers of Christ your mind needs to be renewed daily as you "seek the kingdom of God" and all his righteous (Matthew 6:33). To all the un-saved people (individuals) you need to be born again to be a part of God's kingdom to have eternal life. God Is Love! John 3:16-17 says: *For God so loved the world that he gave his only begotten Son; that whosoever believeth in him should not perish but have everlasting life. For God sent not his Son into the world to condemn the world: but that the world through him might be saved* (KJV).

Although many books have been written about the "kingdom" this book comes at the right time and season, for the right reason which is a call to "repentance" and "salvation" to all mankind whom would believe that Jesus Christ is the only way to receive "eternal life". Ecclesiastes 3:1 says: "To everything there is a season, and a time to every purpose under the heaven". The very word of God you have seen and heard before, "Now Is the Time" take heed, wake up, repent, oh sleeping church and listen to what God is saying through His servant the Prophetess. A time in which many believers are looking for direction while non-believers are seeking and searching for the answer and it has already been revealed. JESUS said, *"I am the way, the truth, and the life no man cometh unto the Father but by me"* (John 14:6). The "kingdom" has come!

This book reveals vital information through the word of God and the importance and urgency of the "Kingdom" which is the ministry of Jesus and how we as believers are to live and function in the earth realm. There are chapters which focus on the Kingdom, a Kingdom Mind-Set, Kingdom-Connectors (five-fold ascension gifts), Kingdom Carrier, Kingdom Assignment, and Kingdom Wealth. This book also includes questions and exercises along with a study guide of scriptures. The revelation of God's word will ultimately change your life and perspective on how you look at the "kingdom" after reading this book and teaching tool, I pray. Jesus is coming back for his bride the church. Are you <u>saved</u>! Are you ready!

Jesus said; *For what is a man profited, if he shall gain the whole world, and lose his own <u>soul</u> or what will a man give in exchange for his <u>soul</u>?* (Matthew 16:26). It is urgent that you repent! And be <u>saved</u>. Now Is The Time!

Ask <u>Jesus</u> to save you now! Romans 10:9 says: That if thou shall confess with thy mouth the Lord Jesus, and shalt believe in thine heart that God hath raised him from the dead, thou shalt be <u>saved</u>.

Chapter 1

What Is The Kingdom?

But seek ye first the kingdom of God, and his righteousness, and all these things shall
be added unto you.
Matthew 6:33

From the beginning of time the bible clearly states God as sovereign, it also portrays Him in conflict with Satan a hostile enemy of the Kingdom. Satan is a ruler of this world (John 12:31, 14:30, and 16:11) and the "god of this age" (II Corinthians 4:4). What is the "Kingdom of God"? And how do we enter in? These questions have been asked by many, and yet there has been many answers given. What exactly does the word "kingdom" mean? According to Webster's dictionary its: (1) the eternal spiritual sovereignty of God or Christ, (2) the realm of sovereignty, and (3) a realm or sphere in which one thing is dominant. The bible speaks of the "Kingdom of God" which is depicted as an entity that always has and always will exist. Psalm 103:19 declares the Lord hath prepared his throne in the heavens; and his kingdom rules over all. This kingdom is an everlasting kingdom, and thy dominion *endureth* throughout all generations (Psalm 145:13 KJV). The devil can do nothing without God's permission (Job 1:12, 2:6). Nothing is outside the perimeter of God's rule.

Now let's take a look at the first mention of the word "Kingdom" used in scripture which is found in Genesis 10:8-10 concerning Nimrod (means relief), who was a mighty hunter in the eyes of the Lord. Here is a man that expressed ideas of God's Kingdom authority, Nimrod was established as a king to rule over the people. The centers of his kingdom were Babylon, Erech, Akkad, and Calneh in Shinar. In the early days of the Old Testament when a man builds a city it becomes his domain or kingdom. The city was walled and usually guarded, and those who lived there paid for their protection, the city offered by being vassals to the chief who was in fact the king. Behind these kingdoms lay a greed of power, control, and wealth which has become a mind-set down through the generations then and now. This record of Nimrod's kingdom is told to us because it reveals the nature of the "kingdom" that was birthed in the heart of man that is set in opposition to the Kingdom of God. It functioned as a totalitarians rule over a people, who are made subservient to a dictator who is accountable only to himself. Jeremiah 17:9 says the heart is deceitful above all *things;* who can know it?

God's "kingdom" must be first (Luke 9:57-60). God's desire is to bring His kingdom here on earth which would take over the systems of this world. God wants us to be salt and light as He uses us to bring forth His kingdom. There is a purpose and plan for God's children here in the earth realm. If you are doing anything else other than living a life that demonstrates the "kingdom" of God here on earth then you are just wasting time. The kingdom of God will manifest here on earth so others will know the truth and the light. Yes, Satan is ruler over the kingdom of darkness and has power but, he is not **all** powerful. God is sovereign and in control, and Satan can only do what God allows. The believer who choose the kingdom of light reflects the spirit of their leader Jesus and those who choose darkness reflects the spirit of their leader, the devil (Satan) who is a murderer and liar (John 8:44).Only Jesus can offer us salvation to the kingdom which is quoted in John 3:16: ***For God so loved the world that he gave his only begotten Son, that*** *whosoever believeth in him should not perish but have everlasting life. Jesus said I am the way, the truth, and the life no man cometh unto the Father but by me* (John 14:6 KJV).

Although the bible has given us information about the kingdom, many Christian believers are still seeking and searching for a clear understanding of how the Kingdom of God applies to their lives. However, we all must understand and realize that the "kingdom" is spiritual in nature although refers to a physical realm that lies into the future. We must not focus on the concept of the physical authority connected with God's kingdom but rather at that which is spiritual. This means as believers we should live and walk in the spirit and not after our flesh (Galatians 5:16).We must live in the realm of the kingdom where we must come in alignment under the direct authority of Christ, which is the Spirit of God dwelling within us.

Jesus and the Kingdom

The kingdom is the gospel, Matthew Chapter 4:23 clearly states: "And Jesus went about all Galilee, teaching in their synagogues, and preaching the gospel of the kingdom, and healing all manner of sickness and all manner of disease among the people. What we can observe earlier in this text at verse 17 the scripture says "from that time Jesus begin <u>to preach</u>, and to say, **Repent: for the <u>kingdom</u> of heaven <u>is at hand</u>**. The word **repent** is found 45 times in the King James Bible. Matthew the only writer of the four gospels that used the term "kingdom of heaven" it is also used 33 times in the New Testament. Mark and Luke used the term "kingdom of God" liberally, but John never used the term "kingdom of heaven". John uses the term "kingdom of God" only two times in his gospel writings. Just as the four gospels are mentioned above Jesus came preaching the gospel of the kingdom after 40 days in the wilderness. In exclusive of this good news is what will happen at Calvary.

The revelation of Jesus life is in the Synoptic Gospels which is found in the books of Matthew, Mark, Luke, and John. Matthew writes to a Jewish audience that Jesus was the Messiah (Christ), the long awaited King of Israel. Mark writes from a Roman perspective (presents Christ as a servant redeemer). Luke the doctor writes to the Greek mind (presents Jesus as the Savior of the World), the intellectual one who is detail trained in the science, and he esteemed the achievement of man. John writes a message to the world about this Jesus the Christ, he lifts Jesus as the Son of God who reigns in the world. The books of Matthew and Luke both gives account on the birth of Jesus Christ. Jesus the Christ in the Hebrew verb means, Savior, one who saves, and Christ the anointed One. The details in the book of Mark gives an account, however it is more graphic in nature than the other Synoptic Gospels yet, the book of John is the only writer who begins his story of Jesus Christ with His external existence rather than the time He appeared on earth. Jesus is the King, long-awaited Kingdom of God.

It is evident when we read the four gospel accounts of Matthew, Mark, Luke, and John and the opening chapters of the book of Acts; the dominant subject is "**the kingdom of heaven**". The prophet John the Baptist prepared the Jews for Christ's teachings by teaching repentance, or turning away from sin, and baptism. The gospel that John the Baptist preached, and the Lord Himself preached, and the twelve apostles were commissioned to preach, was that "**the kingdom of heaven is at hand**". John again gives us another example about the kingdom in John Chapter 3:3-5 when Nicodemus has a conversation with Jesus and Jesus answered and said unto him, *"Verily, verily, I say unto thee, Except a man be born again he cannot see the kingdom of God"*. Nicodemus saith unto him, How can a man be born when he is old? Can he enter the second time into his mother's womb, and be born? Jesus answered, *Verily, verily, I say unto thee, Except a man be born of water and of the Spirit, he cannot enter into the kingdom of God"*.

Now is the Time when Christian believers should be about the ministry of Jesus, the incarnation of Christ teaching, preaching, and healing. All that Jesus did and spoke was related to the kingdom. Jesus knew it was necessary to illustrate/demonstrate the kingdom here on earth. This kingdom would lead us to "salvation" and this is only through Jesus Christ. In John 14:6 Jesus saith unto him, *"I am the way, the truth, and the life, no man cometh unto the Father but by me"*. Those who are following Jesus are to be marked by their love, honesty, integrity, kindness, patience, and willingness to forgive and go the distance for others. Remember the kingdom starts within you.

Jesus enunciated the principles of this kingdom in the Sermon on the Mount recorded in Matthew Chapter 5:3-12 and Luke 6:20-23. Even in the Sermon on the Mount the blessed prospect of the kingdom of heaven was repeated by the Lord for example Matthew 5:3 says: *Blessed are the poor in spirit for theirs is the kingdom of heaven. Matthew 5:10 says: Blessed are they which are persecuted for righteousness sake for theirs is the kingdom of heaven.* This state of blessedness begins the very moment that a person believes on Jesus Christ for salvation (Romans 10:9). This is demonstrated by the fact that the promises concerning the kingdom of heaven in verses three and ten are in the present tense. While in this life one may enjoy the results of these truths, although the ultimate blessedness will be experienced in heaven. Matthew 5:12 Jesus speaks: *rejoice and be exceedingly glad: for great is your reward in heaven for so persecuted they the prophets which were before you.*

Jesus also says, *but seek ye first the kingdom of God, and his righteousness and all things shall be added unto you* (Matthew 6:33 KJV). Have we ever asked ourselves what does this mean? Many Christian believers associate the kingdom (in going to heaven) where we will spend eternity with God and Jesus our Lord and Savior. A place where there will be streets of gold, and angels; a glorious place where there will be no more pain, suffering, tears, death, or sorrows. Yet, the kingdom of God must be shown in our lives here on earth. Jesus said that those who desire the kingdom of God will seek it earnestly and lay hold on it with violence (Matthew 6:33; 11:12). We know that Satan is the ruler of this world system, but God will bring forth His kingdom in the earth realm. As children of God we have a purpose for being here and the sole reason for that purpose is to be used by God to bring forth His kingdom. If you are doing anything other than that you are wasting time.

Many believers today have followed the dregs of society that has an appearance of godliness, but denying the power (have no power). They have given themselves over to mammon, money and the religious gods of this world. Chasing and pursing after their own way to get more and more material success which is the most worthless part of anything that can ever pass for godliness. Have you forgotten what Matthew Chapter 6:33 says? Jesus definitely was about his Father's business, in which His focus was the kingdom of God. This alone indicates how central a position the kingdom occupied in Christ's thought. When he wanted to teach his disciples about the kingdom of God, he did not give them an abstract discourse He told them a story. Jesus told them about the way a farmer sows his seed, the way a fisherman hauls in his catch, about the diamond merchant who sold up to become a connoisseur, and the bandits on the Jericho road.

These stories begin the gospels and continue to the end, explaining, defining, illustrating, and specifying the kingdom of God (Matthew 13:34). Even when Jesus is not speaking in parables, the word **kingdom is seldom absent from his lips,** this expressed the sum context of His preaching, teaching, and His work.

In Luke 17:21 Jesus said, the kingdom of God is within you. The kingdom of God is inside of us if we are born again. Jesus is not speaking about something that is exterior to us but is part of our being. Jesus gives perfect illustrations and examples to make us aware that the kingdom of heaven is liken unto earthly principles and concepts. Through Jesus parables He clearly reveals and shows us how we are to live in the kingdom which is unto heaven on earth. An example of the Our Father Prayer found in Matthew 6:9-13 (KJV) which reads:

*Our <u>Father</u> which art in heaven, <u>Hallowed be</u> thy <u>name</u>. Thy **kingdom** come, Thy will <u>be done</u> in <u>earth</u>, as it is in heaven. Give us this day our <u>daily bread</u>. And <u>forgive</u> us our <u>debts</u>, as we forgive our <u>debtors</u>. And lead us not into <u>temptation</u>, but <u>deliver</u> us from <u>evil</u>. For thine is the kingdom, and the power, and the glory, forever. <u>Amen</u>.*

One day Jesus was praying in a certain place when one of His disciples said to him, "Lord teach us to pray, just as John taught his disciples". Jesus taught them that very prayer above. The emphasis here is "teach us to pray" not how to pray. This is so important what the disciples was asking of Jesus. Have you ever asked the Lord to teach you to pray? Even through this kingdom prayer Jesus was teaching us also that God would provide our daily food spiritually, and physically, forgive us of our sins as we forgive others. Jesus paid the price for all sins through His death, burial, and resurrection. He will lead us not to be tempted from the hands of the enemy devices, because no one can ever truthfully say that God has tempted them to sin.

Many teachings of the **kingdom** were through the parables of Jesus found in the book of Matthew Chapter 13. This is the revelation which I've personally received from these parables. Teaching us the parable of the seeds, how we all have a hidden treasure inside of us and God wants us to use it for the kingdom that is here on earth. The parable of our pearls, what God has given us should not be thrown before swine's, along with the good and bad fish parable which I relate to as the wheat/tares, sheep's/goats that God will separate for the kingdom purpose. Other theologians may look at them from a different mind-set but, this was the revelation that was given to me as someone who studies and seeks after God's word. Even before Jesus, in the days of John the Baptist he came preaching in the desert (wilderness) of Judea saying, <u>Repent</u> ye for the <u>kingdom</u> of heaven <u>is at hand</u> (Matthew 3:1-2 KJV). This is he who was spoken of through the prophet Isaiah. The voice of one crying in the wilderness, "Prepare ye the way for the Lord, make his paths straight". From the days of John the Baptist, the Kingdom has been forcefully advancing. "Now after that John was put in prison, Jesus came into Galilee, preaching the gospel of the kingdom of God, and saying, *the time is fulfilled, and the kingdom of God is at hand: repent ye, and believe the gospel* (Mark 1:14-15).

"These twelve Jesus, sent forth and commanded them saying Go not into the way of the Gentiles, and into any city of the Samaritans enter ye not. *But go rather to the lost sheep of the house of Israel. And as ye go, preach saying, the kingdom of heaven is at hand*" (Matthew 10:5-7 KJV).

The gospel is difficult and many find the kingdom to be controversial and yet Jesus' calls us to follow, which involves speaking out against everyone and everything that hinders God's vision for the world. Why is the gospel difficult? Yet it is the "good news", "kingdom of God" and a word of exhortation and comfort, but before it's a word of exhortation and comfort it's a word of challenge. As we embrace God's vision for His **"kingdom"** here on earth the world puts us at odds with the values of a society that is determined on promoting and organizing itself around the very things that are opposed to God. Just as so many have obsession with wealth and consumerism while ignoring many of the injustice everywhere. When we don't seek the "kingdom" of God first then many believers are susceptible to making other things and other matters more important in life. Then, we will be consoled by it, making Jesus message about the "kingdom" irrelevant because our priority of need makes God a curiosity or just one more commodity to be purchased or controlled by money and material success.

Does our desires to follow the kingdoms of this world for everyone's approval, conforming above all else to the ways of this world, to be socially acceptable, hinder us from following Jesus and advancing His kingdom? Answer the question? Are you willing to be obedient and do what is necessary to advance the kingdom here on earth as gross darkness is seen **everywhere? There is so much that Satan uses in trying to deceive many, which can** lead to not living the kingdom life.

It pleases God when we work together to share the good news about His **kingdom** and advance His **kingdom** here on earth. Know that you have and important part in the body of Christ. Whether you're a minister in the pulpit, or sharing about the kingdom of God on street corners, or whether you sow seeds so that others can go in the mission fields, you are important. Don't ever under estimate the part you play because together we are building the kingdom. Let us spend our lives harvesting a spiritual crop for eternal life. There are endless fields of souls needing to hear the truth, and the **"kingdom"** of God and they are ready "Now Is the Time for the harvest" (John 4:35). The kingdom of God came near and they didn't enter. What a tragedy for the **"kingdom of God"** to come near to you, and you reject it. A truthful witness saves lives, but a false witness is a traitor (Proverbs 14:25).

A Kingdom Divided

The **"kingdom of God"** is love, salvation, compassion, walking in the fruits of the Spirit, and eternal life in heaven. Satan's kingdom will bring you destruction, death and eternal hell. We can't serve God and Satan at the same time. You can't have two masters! You must make a decision! Just as Satan tempted Jesus saying I'll give you all the kingdoms of this world Satan is doing the very same today to those who are authentic in following Jesus and to those who are saying they're following Jesus, but lip service. Luke Chapter 4:5-8 states: And the devil, taking him up into a high mountain, showed unto him all the **"kingdoms of the world"** in a moment of time. And the devil said unto him, All this **power** will I give thee, and the **glory** of them: for that is delivered unto me: and to whomsoever I will I give it. If thou therefore wilt worship me all shall be thine. And Jesus answered and said unto him: *"Get thee behind me Satan: for it is written, Thou shalt worship the Lord thy God, and him only shalt thou serve."* Jesus knew that there was only one all powerful "kingdom" and that is the "kingdom of God".

The kingdom of God is real just as the kingdom of Satan. There is a kingdom of "light" and a kingdom of "darkness". In Matthew Chapter 6:24 Jesus, speaks: *"No man can serve two masters; for either he will hate the one, and love the other; or else he will hold to the one and despise the other; he cannot serve God and mammon."* Joshua 24:15 also states: And if it seem evil unto you to serve the Lord, choose you this day whom ye will serve; whether the gods which your fathers served that were on the other side of the flood, or the gods of the Amorites, in whose land ye dwell: but as for me and my house, **we will serve the Lord**. Amos 3:3 says: Can two walk together, except they be agreed? **Now Is the Time**! You must make a choice on what "kingdom" you are a part of. Satan is the prince of the air but, Jesus is the "Prince of Peace" (Isaiah 9:6 KJV).

Satan is the author of confusion and God is the giver of wisdom, and power. Satan's kingdom is wicked and opposes the things of God. We need to know how to exist in this world while doing the will of the "kingdom of God". He or she who does the will of God remains forever (I John 2:17). We are not to be conformed, fashioned or have a pattern like the kingdom of Satan. We are citizens of the kingdom of God, heirs of the kingdom, chosen generation, royal priesthood, a holy nation, peculiar people: that ye should show forth the praise of him who hath called you out of darkness (Satan's kingdom) into his marvelous light (I Peter 2:9 KJV).

The power of God's kingdom and the power over the devil is taught in Matthew Chapter 12:25-30. Jesus knew their thoughts, and said unto them, *Every kingdom divided against itself is brought to desolation; and every city or house divided against itself shall not stand. And if Satan cast out Satan, he is divided against himself; how shall then his kingdom stand? And if I by Beelzebub cast out devils, by when do your children cast them out? Therefore they shall be yours judges. But if I cast out devils by the Spirit of God, then the* **kingdom of God** *is come unto you. Or else how can one enter into a strong man's house, and spoil his goods; except he first bind the strong man? And then he will spoil his house."* Jesus said to Peter after revelation was given knowing that flesh and blood had not revealed this to Peter in Matthew Chapter 16:17-19. Jesus said to Peter and *I will give unto thee; the keys of the kingdom of heaven; and whatsoever thou shalt bind on earth shall be bound in heaven; and whatsoever thou shalt loose on earth shall be loosed in heaven. The world passes away but "kingdom of God" will stand forever.*

What the Kingdom Is Not!

The kingdom is not all about building churches but **building the kingdom in you** (us). Don't get caught in the paralysis of your analysis of thinking that by going to church faithfully or just on holiday occasions you have come to master what the kingdom is. The kingdom is not about seducing the flock or coercing them with gimmicks or pulling tricks out of your hat through deception of your own doctrine and philosophy, demanding membership roll, condemnation to give offerings and tithes or making your own personal disciples. In many of the churches we have allowed the kingdom to be conformed to the culture and ways of this world. The atmosphere of our own sanctuaries have been polluted by the spirits of sexual immorality, pride, greed, tolerating Jezebel spirits, Babylonians spirit, jealousy, demonic spirits, rebellion, intellectualism, entertainment, all about self-spirit, and everything else that is totally against our Holy God and what the kingdom represents(I Corinthians 6:19).

It is definitely not about the size of a building whether it's a storefront, small, or mega church. Jesus says it so clearly in Matthew 16:18: *upon this rock I will build my church and the gates of hell shall not prevail against it.* Even in this text of scripture Jesus was relating to Peter that the church represents the body of believers here on earth while the kingdom of heaven is made up of both the earthly and heavenly realm. The teaching here is that these things which are conclusively decided by God in the kingdom of heaven, having been decided upon, are emulated by the Church on earth. The church is made up of true believers who acknowledge the deity of Jesus Christ as Peter did. Christ is the "Rock" upon which the church is built (I Corinthians 3:11 KJV). The kingdom is not about prompting your title, educational degrees, positions, or expensive hair or clothing décor it has no bases on what Jesus teaches us about the kingdom.

Paul states that the **kingdom** of God is not meat and drink; but righteousness, and peace, and joy in the Holy Ghost (Romans 14:17). Although these things play a role in the kingdom these views are stated because as believers we cannot allow ourselves to be manipulated by false doctrines, and those who are coming in the apparel of wearing sheep clothing but are truly a counterfeit of a wolf in disguise. Let us as Christian believers therefore not judge those who come to deceive us among the flock but, pray that they may repent and ask for God's forgiveness.

The kingdom is not about how many on the praise team, choir, size of the music ministry (band), wall-to-wall carpet, extravagant chandeliers, or a decorative pulpit although this may be nice to have but are you being effective to those whom are lost and in need of a Savior. Many in the body of Christ have made their Bishop, Pastor, Prophet/Prophetess, and Apostles their little gods. Many are now seeking a man/woman instead of God. They have become such superstars/celebrities and some have fallen because they have been intoxicated with the world's image of success. They have been consumed by the things of this world and have forgotten their first love. All you superstar preachers must come down and humble yourself and as Paul states: "I am just a man"!

Church leaders have allowed the world of familiar spirits to come into the house of God to mock, disrespect, and joke about true spiritual leaders just for entertaining the carnal flesh. Yes! Laughter is good for the soul but at what cost? Leaders have been so politically correct they choose not to confront this type of behavior so they can appease the politically correct crowd. Now Is The Time! Put away all manners of the things that will cause you to displease God and dishonor what the kingdom is about.

The kingdom lifestyle does not include shacking; sleeping around with married or single individuals of the opposite sex or same sex, greed, envy/jealousy, pride, or any other fleshly desires

(James 4:4). Many Christians say they are **saved.** Are you really **saved**? Can you be an effective witness about the Word of God to the one you are shacking with or sleeping around with? What are you going to tell him/her when you are doing the opposite of what the kingdom is all about? Co-habitation staying with one another is not how saved people live or living with an un-saved person (I Peter 1:14-15). The bible also says be ye not unequally yoked together with unbelievers (II Corinthians 6:14).

How can you be with someone who is against your Jesus, God's word, the church and what you believe? Who's been influencing you? Does some un-godly friend or lover has more influence over you than the God whom you say have saved you and you serve? (I Corinthians 5:9-11 KJV). Remember without being holy you can't see the kingdom of God.

Are you a saved Christian? You can't be saved by affiliation or association. Some affiliate with Jesus when they need to and others call on Jesus because of association. This doesn't work! Jesus is your Savior only if you have confessed, believed in your heart that He is the only Son of God. Romans 10:9 clearly states: "That if thou shalt confess with thy mouth the Lord Jesus, and shalt believe in thine heart that God Hath raised him form the dead, thou shalt be saved"; this is the only way to really being **saved** and apart of the kingdom of God. Christians stop deceiving yourselves thinking that you can be a part of God's kingdom without the required changes that must take place in your heart. Remember Satan is trying everything necessary to get you in hell. Avoid the appearance of sin. The kingdom does not conform to the darkness of this world and does not turn off the light to compromise. Now Is The Time! **Repent! Repent! Repent!**

The kingdom is not necessarily all emphasis on preaching and administration of public worship. In fact it's the opposite of what Jesus did. Jesus was a communicator, but He was primarily combining creative teaching, experience personal growth and the work of the Holy Spirit revealing/ creativity to change those who followed him. Jesus is a communicator but, He is also a facilitator. The **kingdom** teaches believers how to grow in relationship, commitment, and obedience to Jesus. This is the essence of how the kingdom is in us out of love, not constraint (John 14:21).

Complacency in the Kingdom

How often do we get complacent because we think we have done enough for the kingdom, or we have to do everything in a big way or not at all and so we opt to do nothing. Have we forgotten that sowing a seed is never a small thing even if only one plant grows from dozens of seeds we have done something for God's glory. Matthew Chapter 28:18-20 has commissioned us all to "go"! Jesus even told his disciples that they will be witnesses in Jerusalem, in all Judea, and in Samaria, and unto the uttermost part of the earth (Acts 1:8). Don't be complacent about pursuing what God has placed in your heart. God is a faithful God! No matter how long it's been, no matter how un-qualified you think you are God has called you to do something in the body of Christ for His kingdom. If not there then where? God can use you anywhere! Use your gift(s) and trust God by faith. Your set time is coming!

Many times things may happen that can lead us to a place of complacency, where we may be going through a trial/test and we need to take a break from doing anything for the kingdom of God. Some may feel just the opposite that they need to be doing something while going through a trial/test but not knowing what to do because they have been complacent for such a long period of time. In the kingdom there should never be a doubt where we feel that we should just sit on the pews or on our padded chairs while others are doing something and we are just looking from afar. There is no time to sit and watch everyone else when you yourself will be accounted for your time spent here on earth. If you are just sitting on the sidelines looking in and not doing what God has told you to do; are you really following His commands? You are in opposition to Him. "But be doers of the word, and not hearers only deceiving your own selves" (James 1:22). Remember as followers and disciples of Jesus Christ we are always needed in the kingdom because the "kingdom is within you"!

Farmers who wait for perfect weather never plant. If they watch every cloud, they never harvest (Ecclesiastes 11:4 NLT). Waiting for the perfect condition or time will mean inactivity. This practical insight is especially applicable to our spiritual life or whatever God has called you to do in the kingdom. If you wait for the perfect time and place for personal bible reading, joining a ministry it will never begin. If you wait for the perfect church, you will never join. If you wait for the perfect ministry you will never serve or get off the pew/chair. Take steps now to grow spiritually. Don't wait for conditions that may never exist. Get up! Get up! Don't let complacency stop you!

Has complacency slipped into your relationship with God? Many Christian believers are complacent because they lose focus. The object of our faith is Jesus Christ alone. Christ and the **"kingdom"** message is our focus. There is no room for complacency in the kingdom of God sitting on padded pews/chairs or the sidelines. Our own spiritual complacency keeps believers from striving toward the great places of the **kingdom** of God.

The Priority of the Kingdom

The greatest teaching and learning you'll ever understand is the priority of the kingdom living on earth. Life on earth holds no greater challenge than the complicating daily demands of choosing what to do, and when to do it. Every day we are making decisions without prioritizing what is important. The kingdom of God was certainly the priority of Jesus Christ. Jesus was about his Father's business to do His will here on earth. Jesus states in Luke 2:49, *"How is it that ye sought me? wist ye not that I must be about my Father's business?"*

Today in the 21st Century most people would look at their priorities as going to work daily so they can have the necessary essentials such as housing, food, clothing, car, and insurance. What a tragedy to think that the basic essentials of life are our driving priorities. God has already promised us these things which Jesus speaks of in Matthew Chapter 6:29-33. Identifying the correct and right priority of the kingdom life is the key to a successful and fulfilled life. Priority can be defined as: putting God first, the principle things, establishing the most important thing, and primary focus. God makes man His first priority, but man makes God his last resort. Seek His kingdom! Make it your first priority. Don't worry about stuff! Don't ignorantly continue to break His commands, study His word and know that you are standing in righteousness. If you do, you'll find all those concerns will fade away and be replaced by the desire of God's (daddy's) heart.

We should be making it our first and most important priority to live according to God's way of doing things in order to have right-standing with heaven. The problem is most Christians don't know God's way of doing things so they just do whatever they feel like doing and say "well I always put God first". Without the Word of God as your source of knowledge when it comes to the kingdom way of doing things you might as well forget those benefits. According to Jesus we are to be seeking and striving after the kingdom's principles and priorities. In Matthew 6:32-34 Jesus is speaking and states: ("For after all these things do the Gentiles seek :) for your heavenly Father knoweth that ye have need of all these things. *But seek ye first the kingdom of God, and his righteousness; and all these things shall be added unto you. Take therefore no thought for the morrow: for the morrow shall take thought for the things of itself. Sufficient unto the day is the evil thereof.*

Many Christian believers must grasp and understand that the kingdom priority involves a prayer life (vertical and horizontal) before God, faith, obedience, and sacrifice. When this is established and lived throughout our daily lives before anything else we can be assured that God will provide the things we need for our daily survival. Certainly, we must see this world from a kingdom perspective and give priority to God being glorified in our home, church, job, community, and our nation. It is our job to be those who manifest the kingdom on earth. We are all commanded to share the "gospel" of the kingdom which means good news. The message of the kingdom is for all people of the earth, those whom would receive and believe that Jesus Christ is Lord. Our priority is to share the gospel of salvation, which says that Christ died for our sins according to the scriptures, and if we will believe and put our trust in Him, He will forgive our sins. As we examine and look to the scriptures we notice that one of Jesus priorities began with His preaching ministry, it was a declaration of the gospel of the Kingdom of God.

Is God really a priority in your life? Life can bring so many things to us which can become so hectic and can cause conflict if we don't learn to prioritize. Have you ever thought that some of the simple things we make as priorities have superseded our God, who many say they love and serve. Here is something to think about! Let's use the cell phone for example and the bible.

- Ever wonder what would happen if you treated your bible like your cell phone?
- What if you carried it around in your purse or pocket?
- What if you flipped through it several times a day?
- What if you turned back to go get it if you forgot it?
- What if you use it to receive messages from the text?
- What if you treated it like you couldn't live without it?
- What if you gave it to kids and others as gifts?
- What if you use it when you traveled?
- What if you used it in case of emergency?

This is something to think about! It makes you go ......hmm........where is my Bible? Unlike your cell phone, you don't have to worry about your bible being disconnected because Jesus already paid the bill with His blood. There are also no dropped calls! It makes you stop and think where are my priorities? When Jesus died on the cross He was thinking of you and I. Were we not a priority to JESUS?

Cell phones have become such a high priority which is due to the aggressive marketing by cell phone companies. Cell phones have become an important part of everyday life. They are no longer viewed as a luxury but more as a necessity. Isn't Jesus a necessity? The cell phone has changed the way people communicate with one another. Where ever you go there is always someone on a cell phone regardless of gender or age. They are either talking/texting whether it's while walking or driving. So many people make it a priority in even choosing a cell phone before purchasing one. Style is the other priority of a cell phone buyer which includes, color, size, ring tones, maker, and carrier of the phone. Cell phones now possess many more features than they did just a few years ago and their capabilities have an impact on our daily lives. Cell phones are important and a priority to many because now days everyone wants communication.

Jesus is always ready and available to all regardless of what color, fashion trends and styles are in. He has all power and capabilities to meet your daily needs and is ready to communicate with you 24/7. Jesus already knows your ring tone and He is the only maker and carrier who gives eternal life. Call Jesus! Make him your priority! Yes! We must prioritize things that are important to us but never ever get so busy we forget why we are really here. As Christian believers God has given us dominion over the earth and we are to take care of what He has given us. We should never neglect our kingdom purpose. Remember why you are here! Stop spending time on consuming more and more things that will not bring glory to God! There are so many distractions that will seduce and hinder you from making God a priority in your life. I definitely understand that a phone is good to have, but have you spent more time on your cell phone than with God?

Jesus said, *"the time is fulfilled, and the Kingdom of God is at hand,: repent ye and believe the gospel"*! Even the kingdom parable acknowledges a small beginning whether it was leaven or a mustard seed that would eventually permeate the whole and result in growth for the kingdom. Now that you've seen different facets of the kingdom, let's take a look at another part of the kingdom which is "servanthood".

The Kingdom of Servanthood

Servanthood is following in the foot steps of Jesus who was a servant (Matthew 20:25-28). "But Jesus called them unto him and said, *you know that the princes of the Gentiles exercise dominion over them, and they that are great exercise authority upon them. But it shall not be so among you, but whoever will be great among you, let him be your minister, and whosoever will be your chief among you let him be your servant: Even as the Son of man came not to be ministered unto, but to minister, and give his life a ransom for many.*

Jesus illustrated a perfect example of servanthood when He washed the disciple's feet. Here we see in John Chapter 13:4-16 where Jesus not only teaches the disciples to serve one another, but also emphasizes the importance of a person being washed spiritually. Jesus is all God who made himself a servant (emptying himself of everything) taking the very nature of a servant to serve others. The Greek word "kenosis" is found in the Epistle of Paul to the Philippians where one can read: "{Christ} who being in form (or nature) of God thought it not robbery to be equal with God: But **emptied** himself taking form of a servant, being made in the likeness of me, and in habit found as a man. He humbled himself, becoming obedient unto death, even to the death (thanatos) of the cross" (Philippians 2:6-8). The term "emptied" in Greek is "ekenosen" that literally means to empty one's self, to become nothing.

Our mind-set must be changed if we are to live a life of servanthood and follow the model of Jesus Christ. Philippians 2:5 (KJV) clearly states: Let this mind be in you, which was also in Christ Jesus. A person cannot enjoy the blessings which results from a close personal walk with Jesus Christ without being spiritually cleansed. We must walk and live in holiness in our service for the kingdom. God commands us to be holy because He is holy (Leviticus 19:2). We can only be holy by the blood of Jesus Christ and the Spirit of God (I Corinthians 6:11, Hebrews 9:14). Our servanthood requires that we have a mind of Christ to walk in obedience, and humility which develops our hearts to serve.

We must also be available to serve when needed if asked. It may also require un-attractive task or duties as taking out the trash, cleaning the bathrooms, mopping floors, or just simply fixing someone else's plate. This should in no way affect our role of serving with a loving and humble heart. The kingdom of servanthood is not just limited to the church but, any and everywhere you have the opportunity to serve others. Those who are in leadership are not exempt from serving and or not required to simply just wait on every opportunity to be served. Paul says that people should be able to observe you and conclude that you are a servant. You don't have to wear a label or hold up a sign to say you are a servant. Paul talked about being a servant of God, while James talks about being a bond servant of the Lord Jesus Christ whom was his half-brother. I Peter 2:18 teaches us that servants be subject to your masters with all fear not only to the good and gentle but also to the forward. (NKJ)

When was the last time you served someone? Have you offered your service to others, whether they were believers or un-believers? Are you a servant that leads or a leader that serves? When was the last time you offered someone a ride in your car that God gave you? Have you offered to help that homeless brother, sister, or family, by sharing your home or even offering to put them up for a night or two in a hotel room? What about the man or woman on the side of the byway/highways who is asking for help? Remember the Parable of the Good Samaritan found in Luke Chapter 10 verses 25-37.

The parable goes:

One day an expert in religious law stood up to test Jesus by asking him this question: "Teacher, what should I do to inherit eternal life?" Jesus replies, "What does the law of Moses say? How do you read it?" The man answered, "You must love the Lord your God with all your heart, all your soul, all your strength, and all your mind, And, "Love your neighbor as yourself." "Right!" Jesus told him, "Do this and you will live!" The man wanted to justify his actions, so he asked Jesus, "And who is my neighbor?"

Jesus then replied with a story:

"A Jewish man was traveling on a trip from Jerusalem to Jericho, and he was attacked by bandits. They stripped him of his clothes, beat him up, and left him half dead beside the road. By chance a priest came along. But when he saw the man lying there, he crossed to the other side of the road and passed him by. A Levite walked over and looked at him lying there, but he passed by on the other side. Then a despised Samaritan came along, and when he saw the man, he felt compassion for him. Going over to him, the Samaritan soothed his wounds with olive oil and wine and bandaged them. Then he put the man on his donkey and took him to an inn, where he took care of him. The next day he handed the innkeeper two silver coins, telling him, "Take care of this man. If his bill runs higher than this, I'll pay you the next time I'm here". "Now which of these three would you say was a neighbor to the man who was attacked by bandits?" Jesus asked, The man replied, "The one who showed him mercy." Then Jesus said, "Yes, now go and do the same". (Cross references: Luke 10:27, Deut.6:5; Luke 10:35, Lev. 19:18).

Would you be able to do what the "good Samaritan" did? Are you really serving in humility? We must always remember the servanthood of Jesus Christ our Lord and Savior. God so loved the world that He gave Christ and Christ so loved the world that He served.

The Bible says that Martha was distracted with much serving, while her sister Mary sits before Jesus feet. No, I'm not suggesting that serving is not important in this statement, but we must be very careful to recognize the difference when there is a time to serve and a time to just simply sit before the Master's feet. Our Christian life is about servanthood. Jesus said, *"But he who is greatest among you shall be your servant"* (Matthew 23:11). Although we must never let anything distract or occupy our time from spending time with God ("daddy") in prayer and studying His word. My prayer is that all in the body of Christ become servants for the kingdom of God. Take this time to ask yourself am I serving in the kingdom? Some may already be serving in the kingdom, but for those who can admit they have not begun their servanthood; What are you waiting for?

In the gospel of Mark he emphasizes Christ's deed not Christ words. Mark shows us what a servant does, not what a servant says. Mark views the death of Jesus as the greatest work a servant can do.

Finally, although the kingdom may involve many aspects throughout your journey of life, remember that God can use you for His kingdom purpose regardless of where you came from. This can only happen when you realize that you are no longer your own and freely surrender all to God. God's purpose for you in the kingdom is greater than you can imagine. Never ever forget what you go through for the kingdom, God is sovereign and in control and will give you the strength to do all things through Christ Jesus. Remember the kingdom is in you!

Chapter 1 Questions and Exercises

1. What does the "kingdom" of God mean to you? When people look at your life does it reflect the "kingdom" of God in you?

2. Are you saved? Are you kingdom connected? Read Romans 10:9 and Romans 10:13 can you identify with these scriptures? Write down whatever the Lord speaks to you.

3. Where is it found in scripture the first mention of the word "kingdom"?

4. Jesus began to preach, and say "Repent; for the _____ of heaven is at hand".

5. What was the prayer Jesus prayed and where is the prayer located in the gospels?

6. Are you sharing the gospel message of the "kingdom" (salvation)? Are you seeking things of the kingdom (eternal) or things of the world (temporal)?

7. As you go forward following the principles and parables Jesus taught what have you learned about the "kingdom of God"?

8. Of the four gospels Matthew, Mark, Luke, and John which writer used the term: "kingdom of heaven"? How many times is the term "kingdom of heaven" used in the New Testament?

9. What are some of the steps you have taken to live a life according to the "kingdom of God"?

10. Read the following passage of scriptures in Matthew 6:24-34 and write down any insight of what this means to you? Also reflect on the following scriptures listed below. Write down your first thoughts after reading these scriptures of text.

*Matthew 4:17

_____

_____

*Matthew 5:20

_____

_____

*Mark 1:15

_____

_____

*Luke 17:20-21

_____

_____

*John 3:3

_____

_____

*John 3:5

_____

_____

"Ask Jesus to save you now and have eternal life". Dear Lord Jesus I repent of my sins; Come into my heart and save me. I believe Roman 10:9 which says: That if thou shalt confess with thy mouth the <u>Lord Jesus</u>, and shalt believe in thine heart that God hath raised him from the dead, thou <u>shalt be saved.</u> For whosoever shall call upon the name of the <u>Lord shall be saved</u> (Romans 10:13).

Chapter 2

A Kingdom Mind-Set

And be not conformed to this world: but be ye transformed by the renewing of your mind, that ye may prove what is that good, and acceptable, and perfect, will of God.
Romans 12:2

We can ask ourselves these questions. What am I thinking? Why am I thinking this? Remember that God knows our every thought. The dictionary tells us that the word mind means: the human consciousness that originates in the brain and is manifested especially in thoughts, perception, emotion, will, memory, and imagination. This involves the collective conscience and un-conscience processes in a sentient organism that direct and influence mental and physical behavior, in which the principle of intelligence; the spirit of consciousness required as an aspect of reality; involving the faculty of thinking, reasoning, and applying knowledge.

The Bible begins with the words "In the beginning". Our natural minds can go no further, for eternity is not of a human concept since we are locked into the limitation we call time, where everything has a beginning and an end. However, we know that at this point in which God created the heaven and the earth. He already existed. As I examine the nature of man we must first realize that man is spirit and flesh. If we are honest with ourselves the first step is to go back to the beginning for only then will we know the truth. In order to understand the truth, we must look at two scriptures and see by the spirit their relationship. The first one is found in Genesis 1:26-27, which details the creation of man. He is declared to be the image and likeness of God, and given dominion over all the works of his hand.

However, the book of John tells us clearly that "God is Spirit, and those that worship Him must do so in spirit and truth". Therefore man, who was created in His likeness and image must be spiritual to have a Kingdom Mind-Set. When man was "formed" it required another act on the

Now Is The Time!

part of God before this man could begin to live. The scripture declares God breathed into man's nostrils the breath of life and man became a living soul (Genesis 2:7 KJV). In Matthew 22:37-38 we see in these scriptures that Jesus said, *"Thou shall love the Lord thy God with all thy heart, and with all thy soul, and with all thy mind, This is the first and great commandment"*. Our thinking is the key to becoming transformed into the Christ image. Through the death of Christ, the human intellect can be transformed into a vessel for loving God. Although we have literally been programmed and conformed to the systems of this world, God has given us the power through the Holy Spirit where our minds can be conformed and transformed by His word.

Even in the book of Genesis Chapter 3:1 the serpent (Satan) temptation of Eve begins in her mind of thinking and questioning did God really say that she could not eat of every tree in the garden? Satan was planting the seed of doubts in Eve's mind. She begins now to reason in her mind of what God said and what Satan is saying. Satan introduces to Eve what the world has introduced to so many believers where everything in the world looks better than what God gives us. The knowledge of God is no comparison to what the world can offer which Satan wanted Eve to believe. The kingdoms of this world offers and teaches that more money, more houses, more cars, more clothes/jewelry, more sex, more fame, status and prestige, and more education will satisfy us. No! No! No! The world knowledge has been so exalted that many think the knowledge of God is of non-affect. With Adam and Eve it started with one thought after the stronghold on their minds. Having all of what the world offers without a renewed mind is just a foolish man with no wisdom. The temptation of the battle in her mind is knowing what is right, but doing what was wrong.

Eve so confused in her thinking gave Adam her husband the fruit that God told them not to eat of. They chose to get their knowledge from another source. The negative deception from Satan led them to think that God was keeping something from them. Once Eve accepted these lies, her desire for the fruit grew until she took of the tree and ate. Eve had made the choice to accept what Satan is offering her and disobeys God's command. Genesis 2:17 states: But of the tree of knowledge of good and evil, thou shalt not eat of it: for in the day that thou eatest thereof thou shalt surely die. (KJV)

Renewing your mind is not an event. You can't have progress as a Christian believer or God's way of success without renewing your mind. Exchange your thoughts and belief to God's thoughts and beliefs. You can pray five times a/day and nothing will happen unless your mind is renewed from your intellectual mind-set of this world. Reading and studying the word of God, meditating on God's word and the desire to eagerly seek Him will lead you into developing a renewed mind. The word of God should be implanted in all Christians believer's lives. The bible is the only manual and road map to a renewed mind. If you don't renew your mind over, and over, and over again you can't affect the Spirit of your mind. The bible teaches us in Ephesians 4:23 which states: and be renewed in the spirit of your mind. The Spirit of your mind affects the habits you do. Change is the process of life. You have to be aware of what you're thinking.

When you want the things of God in life it may cause for some desperation. The blind man in Mark Chapter 10:46-52 was desperate for a change. He was crying out for **Jesus.** Just as he cried out for the change (as the deer patented for water), why not ask Jesus to help renew your mind. Jesus is waiting on somebody, somewhere who is desperate to call His name. Someone who is not satisfied with how their mind has not been totally surrendered to Jesus. Ephesians 4:21-24 teaches us that putting off the old thoughts for new thoughts and the old man for the new man which is after God, change is imminent. When you change your thinking you can change your life.

The Battle for Kingdom Thinking

The mind has always and continues to be in a battle since the beginning of time. Even when Satan deceived Eve in the garden, where she was questioning the very instruction that God told her (Genesis 3:1-8). The battle between believing what God said or the seducing words of Satan, because whoever directs or control our thinking is going to direct and control our lives. When we don't have a kingdom mind-set Satan gets to direct and control our mind, without us realizing it through our emotions, fears, and then he's got us. Deceit and fear is two of the weapons that Satan often uses against believers in the body of Christ. The deception looks real, but is not. When things are bad, and things look worse we must remember that the kingdom of darkness has no power over the kingdom of light. Everything belongs to GOD! When we realize this Satan can use as many of his assigned demons to try to control our way of thinking, but it will not work when we walk in the Spirit. When we allow him in with doubt he will begin to lie and deceive us. II Corinthians 10:5 teaches us that we should cast down imaginations and every high thing that exalteth itself against the knowledge of God, and bringing into captivity every thought to the obedience of Christ.

Romans 12:2 says: Do not be conformed to this world, but be transformed by the renewing of your mind. Did you know that your life will move in the direction of your most dominant thoughts? That's why it's so important to make sure our thoughts are the same as God's thoughts. Whatever you allow into your mind is what will come out in your attitude and actions. The more you meditate on God's word, the more you will transform your thinking to be like Christ. Choose now to focus on the Word of God and allow your mind to be renewed. As you focus on God's thoughts, you will see your attitude and actions become more like Him and you will see His hand of blessings in every area of your life.

Paul teaches us in Philippians 2:5 which states: Let this mind be in you, which was also in Christ Jesus. To ever have the mind-set of Christ you must be born again/**saved** (Romans 10:9). If you are not saved you would never be able to attain the mind of Christ which is through the power of the Holy Spirit. The humble mind-set of Christ in this text of scripture is a command. Paul commands the community to develop this mind-set in your fellowship, which is the only consistent mind-set for those who are in Christ Jesus. Paul is not commanding us to assent to the facts of the matter or the logic of his argument. He is commanding us as a body of believers to live with this "kingdom mind-set" toward one another. We are in Christ. Believers are to become more and more like Christ. The passage in Philippians 2:5-8 is not to simply proclaim truth about Christ and how we must have a mind-set like Him, but the point is that Christian believers must have this same mind-set in our home, community, workplace, etc. The mind-set that existed between the eternal Son and His eternal Father. When Paul outlines Christ's submission throughout the incarnation, he said in relationship with others "your attitude (gk. phroneo) should be the same". Jesus made himself vulnerable to us through submission of His true and whole self; this is how we are to submit ourselves to Him and to others.

Our thought life is the beginning of victory or the beginning of defeat. Our battles are always in the mind. Victories are won and lost here. God's word teaches us about our thoughts and what we should do with them. Proverbs 23:7 says: "For as he thinketh in his heart so is he: Eat and drink, saith he to thee; but his heart is not with thee". When you are going through a battle, or storm you are not going to be victorious if you are always walking in a defeated mind-set. You have no desire to fight because you see yourself as having already lost the battle or been captured by the storm, but it doesn't have to be this way.

God gives us a better way found in Jeremiah 29:11: "For I know the thoughts that I think toward you, saith the Lord; thoughts of peace, and not of evil, to give you an expected end". Our thoughts should be able to reflect the very word of God. Thoughts can become strongholds or they can be steered to the obedience of Christ. II Corinthians 10:4-5 says: "For the weapons of our warfare are not carnal, but mighty through God to the pulling down of strongholds: Casting down imaginations, and every high thing that exalteth itself against the knowledge of God, and bringing into captivity every thought to the obedience of Christ. We must cast down worldly thoughts and replace them with God thoughts. We do this by conforming to a kingdom mind-set which puts our minds and hearts to fulfill obedience.

Some Christians today still choose to have a mind-set that has been adapted by the cultures and systems of this world whether it's political, economical, or technological. Their minds have been so programmed to the systems of this world they continue to base everything on personal opinions, their own facts, theory, intellectual science, psychics, and other false religions doctrine instead of the absolute "truth" which is the Word of God. The media through avenues such as tv, radio, newspaper, internet, billboard advertisements still today have influenced many believers. We've listened to every voice but His voice, and looked at every book but His book (bible). Some believers are not even willing to change the way they think. The kingdom requires you to change by renewing your mind and presenting your body as a living sacrifice which will cause you to see truth and be convicted by the Holy Spirit that dwells within you (Romans 12:1-2 KJV). Some believers desire to continue in their spiritual journey holding onto their carnal way of thinking. These are individuals who say they're Christians, but are not making a greater difference in the world because their standards are no different from the world.

As technology improves, there is much advancement in many different areas which involves our mind and thought process. The systems of this world are constantly providing us with something new to think about, trying to consume our minds with things that get our attention. We must have an understating that our mind must be guarded by not allowing our thoughts to be infected by the toxins of this world system. Christian believers must practice the habit of putting in the right thoughts which only can take place by having a renewed mind. A "kingdom mind-set" is required to replace the carnal thoughts of the flesh.

Our thoughts in the mind is always the road the devil (enemy) travels to get in our lives, whether this is with our family, health, relationships, or job. II Corinthians 10:3-5 states: For though we walk in the flesh, we do not war after the flesh; For the weapons of our warfare are not carnal, but mighty through God to the pulling down of strongholds; Casting down imaginations, and every high thing that exalteth itself against the knowledge of God, and bringing into captivity every though to the obedience of Christ. This is why Romans 12:2 is so vital to renewing your mind.

As believers we must want to think and use our minds for God's glory. Our minds must be renewed by God's word daily. We should buy and read materials that will inject kingdom principles in our minds so our mind-set will begin to pattern itself after positive thinking instead of negative thinking. If your mind is on the things of God, you will be of more earthly good than if it were on the stuff down here. What happens is simple. Some Christians say they are seeking Christ, but are not. They make an outward profession of seeking Christ, but their heart is entirely different. The heart is seeking after material things; after things that will be destroyed; after things that are only satisfying to the flesh, all while the mouth is professing something else. The kingdom of God requires complete allegiance (Mark 8:34-35). Our mind-set is not a partial or part-time allegiance, involving only some of our efforts for a few hours a day, nor does Christ command just one part of our experience, or merely a part of our knowledge. No! He demands that Lordship reign over all (Philippians 2:5-11).

Romans 8:1 says: walk not after the flesh, but after the Spirit (KJV). Walking in the spirit requires a change in your mind-set that lines up with the word of God. Walking in the flesh is a mind-set that lines up with the flesh. The bible says: "For to be carnally minded is death but to be spiritually minded is life and peace" (Romans 8:6 KJV). Remember Satan wants to destroy you with the seducing of your flesh by the things of this world. Sin! has pleasure and it is only for a season. Sin is never free of charge you'll always paid the bill in the end. The wages of sin is death (Romans 6:23). I beseech you my brethren allow the word of God to renew your mind in order for the transformation of a kingdom mind-set by the power of the Holy Spirit. II Timothy 2:15 states: study to show thyself approved unto God, a workman that needeth not to be ashamed, rightly dividing the word of truth.

As mentioned earlier we must cast down worldly thoughts and replace them with God thoughts. We do this by conforming to a kingdom mind-set which puts our minds and hearts to fulfill obedience. The scripture says in Proverbs 23:7: For as he thinketh in his heart so is he: Eat and drink saith he to thee; but his heart is not with thee. The only way for kingdom thinking to control your thoughts is by renewing your mind. In order to take control of your thoughts you obviously have to study God's word and learn to discern what you allow to come in whether through conversations or other avenues. Our minds are constantly running with thoughts. We need to take time to quiet our mind. Our thoughts are powerful which can ultimately determine our behavior whether it is positive or negative. Although the mind is the battle field of warfare our bodies ultimately feels the results. This affects our well being spiritually, physically, and emotionally.

I Corinthians 6:19 states: What? Know ye not that your body is the temple of the Holy Ghost *which is* in you, which ye have of God, and ye are not your own?) Our mind and body are connected. What ever you think can determine what the body does. Many believers struggle with their thoughts not knowing when God is speaking, Satan is speaking, or they themselves wondering what decision they should be making.

We must know God to hear His voice. Christian believers must always remember that God has given us His word to fight the battles in our minds. By, allowing God's word to transform you, kingdom thinking can bring forth a better attitude and a healthy way of living. We have a choice. We've all been given a choice to choose. The world system is different from God's. (kingdom system). The world system is operated by fear and doubt. The world system will never align with the system or kingdom of God. Satan is the ruler over the world system of darkness. The dynamics of a believer's life is found in understanding the Kingdom of God system rather than the kingdom of Satan. Jesus was fully possessed by the Word with the kingdom system. He didn't change His ways to follow the world.

Many Christian want to have one foot in the world and one foot in the kingdom. They are not convinced of what they want and are trapped in the world system with a Jesus jersey on. You have to make a choice it is **urgent**! What system will you choose? It is life or death! **" Now Is The Time**"! Example: A rich man who is dying of cancer is just a poor man in need of a Savior. Only the kingdom of God through the power and blood of Jesus Christ can give you a renewed mind, health, and healing (III John 3:2).

As Christian believers we must exchange our thoughts and belief to God's thoughts and beliefs so we can think and use our minds for God's glory. Our minds must be renewed daily by the word of God. We are salt/light that is different from the world and its cultures. We don't try to fit in the world's way, the world has to fit in our way, and if we don't then we look like the world instead of them looking like the church. Keep in mind again that we should buy and read materials that will inject kingdom principles in our minds so our mind-set will begin to pattern itself after positive thinking instead of negative thinking.

Watch your thoughts they become words.
Watch your words they become action.
Watch your actions they become habits.
Watch your habits they become character.
Watch your character it becomes your destiny.

Characteristics of a Kingdom Mind-Set

A kingdom mind-set involves changing from your old way of thinking to the kingdom way of thinking. It's not just about living the Christian life or abiding by an agenda or following a set of rules. Instead, a kingdom mind-set is characterized by the following:

- Understanding that you are a new creature. II Corinthians 5:17 declares "Therefore if anyone is in Christ, he is a new creation, the old has gone, the new has come!"

- Transforming and renewing your mind. Romans 12:2 says, "Do not conform yourselves to the standards of this world, but let God transformed you inwardly by a complete change of your mind. Then you will be able to know the will of God- what is good and is pleasing to Him and is perfect." GNB.
- Treating others with love. Philippians 2:3-5 says, "Do nothing out of selfish ambition or vain conceit, but in humility consider others both than yourself.

  Each of you should look not only to your own interests but also to the interest of others. Let the mind that is in you be also as the mind of Christ Jesus. GNB.

- Sharing your faith. Matthew 5:14-16 says, you are the light of the world. "A city on a hill cannot be hidden. Neither do people light and put it and put it under a bushel. Instead they put it on its stand; and it gives light to everyone in the house. In the same way let your light shine before men, that they may see your good works and praise your Father in heaven."

When we begin to walk in the spirit of having a kingdom mind-set we understand why we need the 5 Fold-Ascension gifts in the body which Jesus Christ gave us. We can also identify as a disciple of Jesus and share 5 important traits we have developed. These traits are as follows: (1) the disciple chose to submit to the teacher, (2) the disciple would memorize his teacher's words, (3) the disciple would learn his teacher's way of thinking, (4) the disciple would imitate his teacher's life, and (5) the disciple would be expected to make other disciples for the kingdom of God.

A kingdom mind-set does not always mean a life of joyful bliss without ever experiencing trials, tribulation, suffering, or even finding yourself in a wandering wilderness. I Peter 5:8 says: that there is an enemy who wishes to destroy us. "Be self controlled and alert your enemy the devil prowls around like a roaring lion looking for someone to devour." But we also read that Jesus has overcome the world. No matter what opposition you face there is assurance that we can be confident of the relationship with God (daddy), is always with us ready to help us in our everyday tasks. Jesus our Lord and Savior gives us strength to endure and do all things through Him. The power of the Holy Spirit our helper is always there leading us in all truth.

As believers with a different mind-set you don't question your faith, you question your doubt. They don't spend time dwelling on misgiving or expressing faith as an occasional fuel-in-the-pan. They believe God's promises. They guard their thought life because the thoughts are controlled by the Spirit; there is life and peace (Romans 8:6). Practice management of your mind! Scriptures Listed below:

- Philippians 2:5
- II Corinthians 10:4-5
- Philippians 4:7-9
- Hebrews 8:10
- II Timothy 1:7

A kingdom mind-set now involves a new way of thinking, you now choose to contest the strongholds that you will no longer allow to come in and have control and cohabitate in your mind. The thoughts must be challenged by speaking the Word of God to stop them. Your kingdom mind-set must be renewed daily by pouring in and soaking the word of God through a pitcher and a sponge or by any means necessary .Romans 12:2 (KJV) says: "And be not conformed to this world; but be ye transformed by the renewing of your mind, that ye may prove what is that good and acceptable, and perfect will of God". It is of urgency that you allow your mind to be renewed by the word of God, by spending time with Him daily. Christian believers must study and read the word, take time to fast and pray so your mind can be conformed to the kingdom way of thinking. If our minds are not renewed we are susceptible to being deceived when wrong looks right. Guard your spirit and brace yourself for the deceiver. The enemy seizes to deceive more and more. Even the very elect are being deceived by the works of the enemy (Matthew 24:24). Jesus said in Matthew 24:4, *"take heed that no man deceive you"*.

In our pursuit of a kingdom mind-set we must remember it is a process because we are conforming from the old and transforming to the new. It's a life change from the old man to the new man (creature) in Christ. Understand that you are a new creation. II Corinthians 5:17 declares: "Therefore if anyone is in Christ, he is a new creation, the old has gone, the new has come!" Transform and renew your mind. The Good News Bible also gives us a different look of text at the scripture Romans 12:2 which says: Do not conform yourselves to the standards of this world, but let God transform you inwardly by a complete change of mind. Then you will be able to know the will of God, what is good and is pleasing of Him and is perfect".

A kingdom mind-set will not lead you to places where you don't need to go. Psalm 37 :23-24 KJV states: The steps of a good man are ordered by the Lord; and he delighteth in his way. Though he fall, he shall not be utterly cast down: for the Lord upholdeth him with his hand. If you are going to be **saved then** it's time to be **saved** for real, don't play with this. Transformed means change, change, changed, and changed. I'm not here to condemn you I'm trying to help you. We should be able to tell the difference from the Christians who are followers of Christ than the world. If you are willing to show it He may think you're willing to share it. Your mind-set must change! You are **saved** now! Some people make heaven like a piece of cake and their response is Lord, Lord, I've been a member for 30 years, I'm in the choir, music ministry, praise team, speak in tongues, prophesied in your name and yet Jesus said I never knew you. Some believers may have done one of these listed above or several, but yet their mind-set has not changed. Where is the kingdom thinking? Where is the love?

Praying with a Different Mind-Set

Many believers have made prayer a daily part of their lives, spending time with God (daddy) through a vertical and horizontal relationship, while some chose to pray on the run or simply not pray at all. When we spend time with God through a vertical and horizontal relationship we can see the benefits of how we pray and believe in our hearts and mind that God hears our prayers. Even when we don't know what to pray the Holy Spirit gives us utterance. Prayer is the master-key for divine revelation from God. The essence of everything we do must be through prayer. We must come in the prayer of agreement which is the orchestra of God found in (Matthew 18:18-20, and I John 5:4). Agreement is an abstract component. It's invisible not visible. What ever is born of God is tested, tried, and pruned by our faith. We must be tested to be trusted. In I Timothy of Chapter 2:1 he mentions four types of prayers. Here we see supplication-specific request, prayer- all communication with God, intercession-praying for others, and giving thanks-sacrifice.

Jesus preached, taught, and healed but, he also prayed. His prayer life involved praying and fasting, and also communicating with the Father. Jesus is forever making intercessory prayers on our behalf to our Father (daddy) in heaven. In John Chapter 17 this prayer is known as the High Priestly Prayer. Jesus prayer was about glorifying his Father on earth and the finished work which thou gavest him to do. Jesus states in verses 9,10, and11 that he prays for us whom God has given Him because we are God's children and that we become one just as He and the Father are one. Jesus prayer was about unity in the body of Christ coming together on one accord which was God's desire for oneness. When our prayers are based on a kingdom mind-set we will see effective results in our lives and what we do will glorify God our Father. Acts Chapter 2 teaches us regardless of the context of diversity, languages, or cultures when the power of the Holy Spirit came on the day of

Pentecost every believer were filled not just a selected few. This is the fulfillment of Jesus promise to send the Holy Spirit. The purpose of the coming of the Holy Spirit was to glorify Jesus Christ (John 16:7-14 KJV).

Along with the coming of the Holy Spirit, the ascension of Christ itself proves that He had finished the work He had set out to do. When the people of God came together there were miracles.

When our prayers are kingdom minded and on one accord we have the same power through the Holy Spirit to do great and mighty things in the earth realm that will glorify our Father. Just as Jesus prayer was for God's people and the kingdom also the disciple knew how important prayer was. They said, Lord teach us to pray and Jesus said, when you pray say "Our Father"..........which is found in Matthew 6:9-13. Revelation flows from the Father. Peter had tapped into the realm of revelation in (Matthew Chapter 16:13-19 KJV). Through a relationship with God in prayer we as believers can tap into the realm of revelation that reveals truth and receive the keys to the kingdom. Jesus said, to Peter you told me who I am now I'm going to tell you who you are. Peter a true believer who acknowledges the deity of Jesus Christ who is the "Rock" upon which the church is built (I Corinthians 3:11 KJV).

When we come to God in prayer we must come with a clean heart and pure hands. Hebrews 4:16 says "Let us therefore come boldly unto the throne of grace; that we may obtain mercy, and find grace to help in time of need. We then are able to pray from the outer courts, inner courts, and then access the spirit realms into the holies of holies. As we begin to grow and our mind-set has been shifted in the way we pray there is and understanding why the Apostle Paul prayed the way he did. In Philippians 3:10 Paul stated: "that I may know him, and the power of his resurrection, and the fellowship of his suffering, being made conformable unto his death". (KJV)

Our prayer begins when rising up early meeting God in the morning regardless of what time it is. We command our morning decreeing and declaring our day, praying, reading and quoting scriptures, so the oracles of God is coming out of the mouth of God. It's vital we learn to be quiet and hear God's voice and get pass the electricity of things (doctrine) (Hebrews 5:11 KJV). Our hearts and minds must be disciplined to spend time with God in prayer when and wherever He chooses to invite us in. We must have good communication with God. As long as we have an un-cut relationship with God in prayer we will have consistent power because we are connected to the source. Jesus is the true vine. Don't get disconnected! He abides in you, and you in Him. Our consistency and dedication to seek the face of God in prayer allows us to stand with one another as a community of intercessors for the kingdom purpose. We pray to develop the desire to thirst after righteousness through prayer and fasting, and the living word which allows us to grow closer and deeper in our relationship with God.

As the mind of the Christian is transformed, he is able to more easily discern truth from what's false. As the mind becomes more sanctified, it becomes easier to reject arguments, ideas, and assertions that under mind the Bible. Arguments and false doctrines that oppose the Word of God are abundant, subtle, and shrewd. Paul warns us in Colossians 2:8 which states: "Beware lest any man spoil you through philosophy and vain deceit, after the tradition of men, after the rudiments of the world, and not after Christ". Colossians 2:3-5 tells us that Christ "in whom are hid all the treasures of wisdom and knowledge, And that I say lest any man should beguile you with enticing words, For though I be absent in the flesh yet am I with you in the spirit, joying and beholding your order, and the steadfastness of your faith in Christ" we as believers have access to this truth. (KJV)

We are able to discern the different spirits and voice of God. When people are speaking we quiet our spirits to make sure our discernment picks up the frequency. Our spiritual eyes are sharp as and eagle where we see beyond people with fancy suits/attire, money or whatever they have. In our passion to pursue prayer we obtain and understand revelation, knowledge God downloads to us by the Holy Spirit which enables us to beware of things in the spiritual realm. Here listed below are 8 Conditions for Effective Prayer:

- A holy life......................I Peter 1:16, II Kings 4:9
- Faith in God....................Mark 11:22-24, I John 5:14
- Pray in the Name of Jesus....John 14:13-14,26 John 16:23-24
- Boldness.......................Hebrews 4:16
- Forgiveness....................Matthew 6:14-15
- Be Consistent.................Matthew 7:7-11, Luke 18:1-8
- The Will of God...............I John 5:14
- Unity..........................Matthew 18:19-20

When we choose to desire and pray kingdom principles, to live and love God with all our mind, we will be fit for the kingdom. If you and I "worship Him with all your mind" the scripture says, "ye shall in no wise be cast out and the hope of his glory and of eternal life [shall] rest in your mind forever (John 6:37;40 KJV). If you will turn to the Lord with full purpose of heart, and put your trust in Him, and serve Him with all diligence of mind, He will deliver you. We occupy our minds doing kingdom business in a worldly system, not allowing our thoughts to be infected by the toxicants of this world. If we get in the habit of putting in the right thoughts this is how our minds are renewed with thoughts of love, faith, hope, encouragement, and patience. Detoxify all the garbage, low self-esteem, fear, despair, and any negative thinking that will hinder your renewing of the mind.

When our minds have been shifted from asking God to do this or telling Him I want this, our focus and desire when praying to God begins with our worship, praising God for who He is, asking for forgiveness, which then allows us to enter in. We must come to God in spirit and truth. Let's begin with entering the gates, the outer court, then the inner court (holy place) and we now then have access to the holy of holies. The phase of entering the gates is intended to be "horizontal". Enter into his gates with thanksgiving and into his courts, with praise, be thankful unto him, and bless his name (Psalm100:4). It is called to everyone to come into the presence of the Lord and prepare himself/herself for worship. The outer court was accessible to all. It represents our visible life (body) and in the place of external worship.

As a person enters the temple he goes further until he confronts the altar of sacrifice, the place where the Son of God serves as our personal and corporate substitute. The outer court was the area of ceremonial washing. This represents the ministry of the word of God exposing and cleansing our actions that do not conform to God's standards. The holy place was only accessible to the priest. The pieces of furniture within the holy place represent priestly duties and demonstrates why it represents the soul. The lampstand represents the light of the word of God; the shewbread represents the place of fellowship/communion, and the altar of incense represents the place of prayer and intercession. Furthermore, all of the furniture in the holy place is made of gold. The holy of holies was accessible by the high priest one day per year, it is the secret place of the most high, and so the Holy Spirit indwells the spirit man (in those who believe). Without the presence of God there was no light in the holy of holies, a fitting metaphor for the dormancy of fallen man's spirit (John 8:12; 6:35; 17:3). As Christian believers you have access to go into the different phases of entering in and seeking a stronger and more intimate prayer life with God as He lives in you. Jesus the great High Priest has come so that they (their names) may have life; even eternal life, and have it abundantly (John 10:10 KJV).

Prayer is so vital in our lives when we go through spiritual battles. Prayer is what builds you up in the Spirit. When you pray you have power, more prayer more power, little prayer, little power and no prayer no power. Paul tells us how we wrestle not against flesh and blood, but against principalities, against powers against rulers of the darkness of this world, against spiritual wickedness in high *places* and about the Christian (whole armor of God) armor in Ephesians Chapter 6 verses 10-18 (KJV), your fight and struggle will always be in the spirit realm. The battle is not in the flesh whether it is at home, work, school, or the church. The battle will always be about righteousness and un-righteousness.

The battle is between light (phos) and darkness (skotia). Winning the battle in your mind can only be done through knowing God's word which is through prayer, studying, and living according to the Holy Scriptures in which God has given us the manual to follow, the Bible (basic instructions before leaving earth). When we pray with a different mind-set we allow the Holy Spirit to come in and make intercession; for us with groaning which cannot be uttered (Romans 8:26 KJV). He knows our infirmities and inability to articulate what we feel when we're praying. When we are praying in a language we don't know and the words of the prayer is not cognitive by mind it's speaking through the spirit. Prayer should be done at any given time in our life whether it's verbally or not. In every season in our life we are to stay connected with God through praying.

Christian believers are often in the same predicament as people of this world. We live in a dimly lighted world, where sin is the rule and there is no expectation to do right and some believers get accustomed to this mind set, but yet we are supposed to be children of the light. We must always be on our guard that we do not become so accustomed to the darkness of this world that we think it is normal and conform to its guidelines. It is not normal! The dim moral and spiritual insight of the world is not the standard that the Christian believer is to walk by (Matthew 5:13-16). We should come up to God's standards rather than think God should come down to ours, which will never happen. Un-believers of this world are proud, self-sufficient, and do not understand their own unrighteousness before a Holy God. Before we can discuss how a believer can influence the world, we have to examine what type of people are believers. Jesus described these people in Matthew 5:3-12, we have come to know these verses as the Beatitudes. These are basic character traits of the kingdom which Jesus teaches us in the Sermon on the Mount, calling for humility, willingness to suffer for persecution, a life of prayer, prioritizing spiritual matter over material things and an earnest attention to God's commandments as believers of the kingdom.

God wants us to use these godly character traits which will develop us as believers through the Holy Spirit, who distributes gifts of power for kingdom service. Our creative thoughts are now established from God with sustainability in life from something the Creator gave the creation in life. Our minds are to be just as Christ so as believers we must pray like breathing in and out, spend time with God (daddy) so we are able to love, forgive, walk in humility, serve others, and show compassion to others. This can only be done through the Christ in us. Jesus is our supreme example. We must be fruitful and multiply as we do kingdom business because **Now Is the Time** for the saints to possess the kingdom here on earth. This is your day, this is your time; be "kingdom" minded. Through our kingdom mind-set we believe the promises of God and know that He hears our prayers because Jesus our Great Intercessor is praying to the Father on our behalf. Amen!

<u>Chapter 2 Question and Exercises</u>

I. Read Romans 12:2 and Philippians 2:5 and answer the following questions listed below:

1. What do these passages of scripture teach you about having a mind-set change?

2. Is your mind being transformed on a daily basis?

3. Do you tend to dwell on more positive thoughts or negative thoughts?

4. Are you "kingdom minded", doing the things of God or worldly minded doing the things that are contrary to God?

5. Jesus said in Matthew Chapter 22:37, "Thou shalt love the Lord thy God with all thy heart, and with all thy soul, and with all thy mind. Do you love the Lord the way Jesus describes in this text of scripture?

II. Read Romans 8:7; II Corinthians 10:5, I Timothy 6:5, II Timothy 3:8 and answer the following questions:

1. What does Paul and timothy teach you about these scriptures? How important is it to have a mind of Christ?

2. How do you respond when un-godly thoughts come into your mind?

3. Where in scripture does the bible say: "For my thoughts are not your thoughts, neither are your ways my ways, saith the Lord.

4. Job 22:13 says: But he is in one _____, and who can turn him? and what his soul desireth, even that he doeth.

5. Philippians 2:2 says: Fulfill ye my joy, that ye be _____, having the same love, being of one accord, of one mind.

III. Can you list the characteristics of having a "kingdom mind-set" found in this chapter? List them below.

1. _____

2. _____

3. _____

4. _____

5. _____

The question was asked to Jesus, which is the greatest commandment in the law? Write those two commandments in your own words from memory. Now look in your bible to see what you have written. Do you have a kingdom mind-set to fulfill these commandments? Matthew 22:36-40

_____

_____

Praying with a different mind-set is crucial for you to live the kingdom life here on earth. Summarize in your own words what you have learned from Chapter 2 "Kingdom Minded? Do you desire to be Christ like-minded? Are you willing to have your mind transformed to the things of God?

_____

_____

"Ask Jesus to save you now and have eternal life". Dear Lord Jesus I repent of my sins; Come into my heart and save me. I believe Romans 10:9 which says: That if thou shalt confess with thy mouth the <u>Lord Jesus</u>, and shalt believe in thine heart that God raised him from the dead, thou <u>shalt be saved</u>. For whosoever shall call upon the name of the <u>Lord shall be saved</u> (Romans 10:13).

Chapter 3

Kingdom-Connectors Five-Fold Ascension Gifts

And he gave some apostles, and some prophets, and some evangelists,
and some pastors and teachers.
Ephesians 4:11

The vital aspect of this chapter is to maintain the importance and distinctions between the five-fold ministries known as the ascension gifts of Christ. These gifts are different from the other two of the three primary gifts which are: (1) the ascension gifts of Christ (Ephesians 4:7-8-11) also called the five-fold ministry, (2) the functional gifts of God (Romans 12:3-8) also called the motivational gifts, and (3) the gifts of the Spirit (I Corinthians 12:4-10) also called the manifestual gifts.

The ascension gifts of Christ are the leadership offices of the church. These five gifts were given to the church by Christ when He ascended into heaven for the purpose of taking over leadership of the church. They are gifts of spiritual leadership and authority that have been given according to the grace of God; not office or positions of governmental authority that have been instructed by man, which are the office of overseer, elder, and deacon. These gifts must be imparted, activated, and directed by the Holy Spirit. The ascension gifts of Christ are: the apostle, the prophet, the evangelist, the pastor, the teacher (Ephesians 4:11).These kingdom-connectors must fully be operating and working together in a cooperate body for the kingdom of God.

The ascended Christ is the head of the church, and these five fold gifts of ministries are His five leadership models for the body of Christ. Even today we as believers must see that in order for the "kingdom of God' to be effective we must allow the Holy Spirit to move throughout the body in which individuals with their gifts can function. Although these gifts are important Kingdom Connectors ascension gifts they are not perfect and should not be worshiped. Those who have these individual gifts must die to their flesh and be changed and live/walk in the Spirit like everyone else.

They must not become so focused on their gifts that they lose sight of their own imperfections. The gift is separate from the person. They must receive ministry as much as anyone else so that they can be perfected.

Many of the five-fold gifts have been wrongly used in teaching or practice in the body of Christ, which has caused much confusion within the gifts. Remember the gifts all work together for perfecting of the saints. The "five-fold ascension gifts" are to build up the saints and lift them up. This should be one of the main purposes of the church. The five-fold ascension gifts are in an individual, it is a calling from God, not a decision of man. It is a gift given by Christ, not an ordination approved by man. Ordination should only be for the purpose of confirming this gift and calling. These gifts are not one you take upon yourself to take a higher position (Luke 14:7-11). It is a gift and office that only Christ can give to you.

The "ascension gifts" based upon Ephesians 4:8, 11 says: "wherefore he saith when he ascended upon high, he led captivity captive, and gave gifts unto men… and he gave some apostles; and some prophets; and some evangelists; and some pastors and teachers. The five-fold ascension gifts are based upon the doma gifts. The word "doma" comes from the Greek word "gifts" used in Ephesians 4:8. These doma gifts did not come into the Church until Jesus ascended (hemue) the term "ascension gifts". Before this time, there were apostles, prophets, and teachers, but they were not "doma" gifts to the church; they were gifts from the Old Covenant. There is definitely a relationship between the ascension gifts of Christ and the functional gifts of God. The relationship is that each ascension gifts correspond to one of the functional gifts. The Apostle core gift of ministry of managing, the Prophet core gift of ministry is prophecy, the Evangelist core gift of ministry is mercy, the Pastor core gift of ministry is encouraging, and the Teacher core gift of ministry is teaching.

Let's take a closer look and the thumb will represent the (5) five-fold ministry:

Apostle: is the thumb. ministry of managing.
Prophet: is the pointer finger (prophetic message for your life, points the way forward).
Evangelist: is the middle finger, which shares the Word.
Pastor: is the ring finger, straight to the heart. Shepherd loves to shepherd you.
Teacher: is the little finger, cleans out the wax.

These ministry gifts are for the purpose of leading the church and perfecting the saints into a spiritual maturity and a work of ministry for the building up the body of Christ. They are office ministries called five-fold "ascension gifts" since these ministries are of leadership and authority. The significance of Christ ascending and descending is "that He might fill all things" and have authority in both heaven and earth (Romans 10:6-7, Ephesians 1:7-23, Colossians 1:9-20). As we examine in scripture Christ himself, being the Apostle (Hebrew 3:1) the Prophet (John 6:14), the Evangelist (Mark 1:14-15), the Pastor (I Peter 2:25), and the Teacher (John 13:13-14) of the church.

The ascended Christ is the head of the church, and again you must remember these five fold gifts of ministries are His five leadership models for the body of Christ.

According to many encyclopedias, a hand is formally called the dorsum of the hand (back of the hand). The thumb (connected to the trapezium) is located on one of the sides, parallel to the arm. The thumb can be easily rotated 90 degrees, on a level perpendicular to the palm, unlike the other fingers. The human hand consist of a broad palm (metacarpus) with five digits, attached to the forearm by a joint called the wrist (carpus). The four fingers on the hand are used for the outermost performances; these four digits can be folded over the pal which allows the grasping of objects. The **thumb and each fingers** works very effectively for its purposes. Each finger, starting with the closest to the thumb, has a colloquial name to distinguish it from the others:

index finger (med./lat. digitus)
middle finger (med./lat: digitus me`dius and more commonly digitus tertius)
ring finger (med./lat: digitus annula`ris) annulus
little finger (med./lat: digitus mi`nimus ma`nus) or pinky-mininus

The hand according to Webster's dictionary is the terminal part of the human arm located below the forearm, used for grasping and holding and consisting of the wrist, palm, four fingers and opposable thumb. The hand as an instrument for making or producing, the hand as a symbol of promise, skill or ability to work with the hand is some reasons why the hand must use the thumb and four fingers to work effectively for the task to be completed. As we examine the hand and its importance from the perspective of what the encyclopedia and dictionary states it is very clear how the hand plays a very vital role on the human body. Each of the fingers has unique cultural and functional significance. For the church today to be powerful and effective, they must reactive the ministries of the Apostles, Prophets, Evangelists, Pastors, and Teachers.

The **five-fold ministry is like the five fingers of a hand**. If we had a hand with only three fingers we can use it but it is not ideal. The handicap is obviously there when we want to use it for a heavier task. The church today is heavy in its task so it is of urgency that we restore the complete operation of the five-fold ministry by giving the rightful positions of the Apostles, Prophets, Evangelists, Pastors, and Teachers.

Even today as believers we must see that in order for the kingdom of God to be effective we must allow the Holy Spirit to move throughout the body in which these gifts can function. Although these gifts are important kingdom connectors ascension gifts all are not perfect and should not be worshipped. Individuals who have these gifts must live a holy life style, die to their flesh and be changed, live and walk in the Spirit like everyone else. As stated earlier they must not become so focused on their gifts that they lose sight of their own imperfection. The gift is separate from the person. They must receive ministry as much as anyone else so that they can be perfected. Many of the five fold gifts have been wrongly used in the body of Christ which has caused much theological disagreements, and confusion within the gifts. Remember, the gifts all work together for perfecting, of the saints. Ascension gifts are supposed to build up the saints and lift them up. This should be one of the main purposes of the church.

The five fold ascension gifts which we find listed in Ephesians 4:11 are given by Christ which allows the nurturing and equipping of His church. These gifts are not for ecclesiastical competition or hierarchical control. Here are several indicators in the calling of an ascension gift or five fold ministries that is listed below:

1. There is a burden, to lead and equip the people of God.
2. God will speak into your heart and call you to this ministry.
3. God will have to prepare you for this ministry and you may feel that the calling is too big for you.
4. If the gift is not evident at first, the gift will come forth and there will be an effective and increasing anointing upon your life. (ministry)
5. God will confirm the calling by others in the body of Christ.

I Timothy 4:14a says: "Do not neglect the gift that is in you" (NKJV) and II Timothy 1:6 says: "Therefore I remind you to stir up the gift of God which is in you through the laying on of hands. (NKJV)

During my study of scripture in the Old Testament of Numbers Chapter 27 there is a story of the five daughters of Zelophehad which can be related in some contextual experience to the five-fold ministry. Their names are Mahlah, Noah, Hoglah, Milcah and Tirazh. Zelophehad daughters according to the Hebrew Bible lived during the Exodus of the Israelites from Egypt; they raised before Moses the case of their rights and obligation to inherit property in the absence of a male heir in the family. These women were wise, Torah students, righteous, and were determined to stand for what was right. They were connected with different gifts and yet were used to effectively work together for a kingdom purpose. The five different gifts reflect what role they each played in their assignment which brought forth their inheritance. When the five-fold gifts are used correctly in the body of Christ the power of God is manifested through salvation, healing, deliverance, and miracles (signs and wonders).

The significance of how important these gifts are should never be taken lightly and should be operating in the body of Christ. Here is some important biblical information on each of the " five ascension gifts" and <u>their role of office in the body of Christ.</u>

Apostle – (Greek: apostolos) someone sent out with a message or as a delegate according to the Synoptic Gospel (i.e., the Gospels of Matthew, Mark, Luke, and John whom Jesus had chosen in order to send them on a specific mission (assignment). In the case of Paul, numerous scriptures state that he was "called to be an Apostle" ten of his epistles begin with a statement acknowledging his call to be an Apostle (for example Ephesians 1:1; Colossians 1:1). Paul exhibited the fruit of an apostle; yet he also held an evangelistic journey and itinerated from church to church. He pastured for several years and churches were established out of his ministry. He taught the word of God and wrote fourteen divinely inspired letters that became books of the New Testament. Despite these ministries, he never states that he was called to be a Pastor, Teacher, Evangelist, or Prophet. He does declare that he was ordained as an Apostle to be a preacher and a teacher of the Gentiles (I Timothy 2:7; and II Timothy 1:11).

The fact remains, that though Paul did the ministerial work of evangelizing, teaching, pasturing, and even at times he functioned like a prophet he had never forgotten he had one Christ-gifted calling that of the Apostle. Each ministry has one specific gifted calling but may perform many of the five-fold ministerial functions. Biblical characteristics and ministry of Apostles can be found in the following scriptures: Acts 2:4; 2:14-36; 3:1-8; 4:1-12; 5:1-11; 5:12; 5:42; 6:1-6; 8:14-17; I Corinthians 3:10; I Corinthians 4:14-15;

Ephesians 2:20; 3:3-5; 4:11-12; and these are just a few of many scriptures that can be found in the bible clearly stating the role and function of an Apostle in the body of Christ.

The "apostle" (the one who is sent) can be applied to a messenger who is sent on a mission in the New Testament. An apostle is a person who is sent out to establish a new church. This is what happened in the church in Antioch (Acts 3:1-3). In this church there were prophets and teachers. When they were at prayer, the Holy Spirit told them to set aside Paul and Barnabas to be apostles. After this occurred Paul and Barnabas then journeyed through Asia Minor establishing new churches. This is the ministry of the apostle. The apostle's journey may not necessarily go very far. Often at times they may go to a place where there are already some converts (Acts 16:11-15). They will go where ever the Spirit is moving. Knowing and hearing the voice of God will be very important in knowing where to go.

In today's 21st Century apostles are still being sent out by Jesus to carry His message. Apostles are an important part of the numbered five fold ascension gifts ministries in Ephesians 4:11 along with prophets, evangelists, pastors, and teachers. When these gifts are effectively used we all will come in the unity of the faith. When apostles are sent to go they go in the name of the one who sent them. Jesus told his disciples "Listen! I am sending you out just like sheep to a pack of wolves. You must be as cautious as snakes and as gentle as doves" (Matthew 10:16 GNB). In the text of scripture Jesus was used the Greek word "apostle". In Matthew Chapter 10 when Jesus chose the twelve apostles they were commissioned by the Lord which was given special instructions and they were to focus their ministry on the Jews (Matthew 10:1-15).

In Luke 22:35-36 the Lord sent his disciples on an extended mission to the Gentiles and gave them instructions that were in direct opposition to what He gave in Matthew Chapter 10. The scripture also gives us another example where Jesus sent out the seventy in Luke 10 verses 1-5. It is so crucial to follow the instructions we are given by the Lord when we're sent out.

Apostles should never be sent out alone. Even a mature Christian like Paul had others with him for protection. This helps to provide protection from human errors and others can help pray in the spirit realm against the attacks of Satan. Sending a person along to start a new church is like sending a troop of soldiers armed with a bat to fight against an arsenal. Apostles break new ground, this is why they are listed first in (I Corinthians 12:28). The example of Paul is in I Corinthians 4:9-10. An "apostle" will set standards for the church according to divine mandate. Every church must be founded on a solid foundation of holiness and righteousness so there would be good prophetic insight from the beginning. An apostle does not rest on his laurels. After the new church has grown to maturity, there will be and apostolic team sent out.

Many times the apostle is always accompanied by a prophet. The prophet would impart vision and zeal into the new church. This is why a church is said to be built on the foundation of apostles and prophets (Ephesians 2:20). Although the other three gifts are just as important in the five-fold ascension gifts. The bible states in Acts 15:32 that Silas the prophet and Barnabas son of encouragement (Acts 4:36) both accompanied Paul on the journey. Even when Paul and Barnabas had a disagreement, Paul would not go out until he had found another prophet (Silas), which was help for the assignment at hand.

"Evangelist Billy Graham used the word "apostle" in three senses. First, apostleship is used in a general sense that all of us are sent into the world by Christ. The second use is the messengers were sent on particular errands. The third is the gift of apostleship".

<u>Some apostles mentioned in the New Testament are:</u>
1. The Seventy (Luke 10:1,3), Matthias (Acts 1:26)
2. James , the brother of Jesus (Galatians 1:19)
3. Paul (Acts 14:14)
4. Barnabas (Acts 14:4; 14), (I Corinthians 9:5)
5. Apollos (I Corinthians 4:6-9)
6. Titus (II Corinthians 8:23)
7. Timothy (I Thessalonians 1:1; 2:6)
8. Silas (I Thessalonians 1:1; 2:6)
9. Andronicus (Romans 16:7), Junia (Romans 16:7)
10. Epaphroditus (Philippians 2:25)

We must beware that there are also "false apostles" whom the Lord has not sent but go anyway. Many of us may have heard these words some were called, some were sent, and some just went. There are false apostles, ones that look and act like the real thing has both subtle and glaring differences. As Christian believers we need spiritual discernment to recognize them. Jesus commanded the church of Ephesus in the book of Revelation to John who wrote, *"I know thy works, and thy labor, and thy patience; and how thou canst not bear them which are evil: and thou hast tried them which say they are apostles, and are not and hast found them liars"* (Revelation 2:2 KJV).

False apostles operate through manipulation and control in order to maintain a following while true apostles will display true servanthood and humility. We are not to be deceived by following false apostles or persuaded toward a doctrinal spirit that drives us. Jesus told us not to!

Since the recognition of true apostles is found in the prophetic spirit, many groups such as skeptics, fundamentalists, other religious groups, and cults deny the existence of modern day apostles. True apostolic authority lies in the collective consciousness of truth. As we allow the Holy Spirit in leading ministries to establish unity through us, as we submit to the Lord. The apostle has authority which comes out of relationship with the body of Christ. Paul demonstrated this type of authority in his epistles. He was able to give direction to the churches because he had a relationship with them. Paul was the "apostle" who had established their church. This authority Paul had is completely different from the world's model. It does not depend on legal power or position which is a worldly system. Paul has kingdom authority! True spiritual authority will be a **threat**, just as it was to the religious leaders in Jesus day. Apostles will always be a part of the five fold ascension gifts that Jesus Christ gave to the body of Christ. Apostles should be ready and available to go when and wherever God leads them for the purpose of the body of Christ. An apostolic calling today should be given to bring churches together more instead of focusing on establishing more new buildings.

Prophet – (Greek: prophetes) used in the Septuagint to translate the Hebrew word nabi` probably meaning "one who utters a God given message". The word originally meant forth teller but came early to encompass the ides of foretelling; and both ideas forth-telling and foretelling are properly associated with the term Prophet. A **prophet** is one anointed to perceive, to speak the specific mind of Christ (church, nations), a teller, proclaimer, interpreter as the oracles of God. A prophet is a seer but every seer is not a prophet. The role of a prophet who has been called by God is strictly a gift from Christ Himself. Jesus was able to receive the mind and power of God his Father and know what was in the heart of human beings through His office of Prophet (John 21:15-23). When Christ Jesus calls and gifts a man or woman with that part of His ability, attributes, and divine nature then that person has been commissioned to the office of prophet. A person cannot call or appoint themselves to any of the five-fold ascension gift ministries.

Prophets will have the ability to prophesy. They will vary in their gifts of the Holy Spirit, but they primarily move in the gifts of prophecy, word of knowledge, word of wisdom, discerning of spirits, and sometimes healing. The typical prophet moves more in prophecy, word of knowledge, and word of wisdom. The first mention of a prophet in the bible is referenced in Genesis 20:7 in which God said to Abimelech, king of Gezar, concerning Abraham, "he is a prophet". Moses was a prophet truly in a classic sense. There were other great prophets like Elijah and Elisha, Isaiah, Jeremiah, Ezekeil, Daniel, Hosea, Amos, Jonah, Micah and John the Baptist, and many, many more were people of mighty words. The great prophets of biblical times were driven by an irresistible constraint to declare the Word of the Lord and to act in response to the Word of the Lord.

Jesus Christ our Lord himself was a "prophet" mighty in deed and word before God and all people". Reference to the following scriptures: Matthew 21:11; Luke 24:19; John 4:19; John 7:40 and His most profoundly prophetic witness to the world was His incarnation. **Jesus Christ was a Prophet of prophets**.

Prophecy is the work of a prophet, the vocation of a prophet, and the utterance of a prophet. It can be described as courageous, a form of bold communication, or a cathartic prophetic art. It may be a prediction, discernment, and interpretation of the signs of the times (Matthew 16:3). Ministers and other believers who are not called to the five-fold ascension gifts may manifest one or more of these gifts, but there is a difference in their anointing, and authority. A believer manifesting the gift of prophecy to a congregation is limited to the general activity of that gift which is edification, exhortation, and comfort (I Corinthians 14:3). When the prophet or prophetess is ministering through his or her gifted office the prophetic anointing has the same authority for reproving, correcting, directing, and instructing in the rhema Word of the Lord as the other four ministries have in teaching, counseling, and preaching, with the Logos "word".

The word nabi` and hozeh are close synonyms, in Amos 7:12 which reads: "Also Amaziah said unto Amos, O thou seer go flee thee away into the land of Judah, there eat bread, and prophesy there". Amaziah calls Amos "hozeh" but suggests that he prophesy in Judah (verb naba` from same root as nabi`) while in Ezekiel 13: 9 the noun verb hazah has "prophet" as its subject and in Isaiah 29:10 nabi` and hozeh are in parallel. Just as we take a closer look at Amos the herdsman, yield reluctantly to heed God's call to "go" prophesy to my people" (Amos 7:15). He declares, "The Lord has spoke; who can but prophesy?" (Amos 3:8). Amos also declares that "I am not a prophet, nor a prophet's son; but I am a herdsman, and a dresser of sycamore trees, and the Lord took me from following the flock" (Amos 7:14-15). In other words Amos doesn't want to be classified as a professional prophet.

As for Isaiah, the aristocrat, he voluntarily accepts God's call as a spokesman. Isaiah was worshiping in the temple, he hears the voice of God speaking; "whom shall I send, and who will go for us?" (Isaiah 6:8). He replies: "Here I am! Send me." God answers: "Go, and tell this people, "Hear ye indeed, but understand not: and see ye indeed, but perceive not" (Isaiah 6:9). In Chapter 6 of Isaiah it presents God's calling of Isaiah, although some see this as Isaiah's initial call to his prophetic ministry. Isaiah's call began with a vision of God's holiness (vv.1-4). Just like Jeremiah (Jer.1:17-19) and Ezekiel (Ezek. 2:3-7), Isaiah was commissioned to speak to obstinate people who rejected God. The words of Isaiah's commission (Is. 6:9-10) were used repeatedly by Jesus in the New Testament to explain why He taught in parables. (Matt. 13:14, 15; Mark 4:12; Luke 8:10)

Jeremiah learns that he was appointed a prophet to the nations even before he was born (Jer.1:5). The content of Jeremiah Chapter 1 discusses the signs which authenticated Jeremiah's calling. He complained that he is young and does not know how to speak, God touches Jeremiah's mouth and says: "Behold I have put my words in thy mouth" (Jer.1:9 KJV).

Some prophets are primarily spokesman to their own generation; the prophets tackle the current issues of the day. However they are interpreters of the past telling God's acts in dealing with the people as a way of revealing divine history. Example, Jeremiah attributes Jerusalem's fall to Israel's idolatry (Jer.44:2-6) and God's wrath on the wickedness of Shiloh is to be Israel's fate (Jer.7:12-15). The prophets are also predictors of the future, near and distant to some extent. Amos was one for example who predicted the imminent Assyrian invasion of western Asia and the conquest and downfall of Israel (Amos 7:7-8). Nahum who wrote the phrase "burden of Nineveh" he was referring to his prophecy concerning Assyria's destruction and the removal of their oppressive hand on the people of Judah. Micah, in 700 B.C. foresees the birth of Christ in Bethlehem (Micah 5:2; cf. Matthew 2:2-6). We must also remember that both true and false prophets operated in Israel just as they operate today throughout the world.

Prophetess- (prof`-et-es, nebhi`ah; prophetis) The first mention of the word prophetess is in the book of Exodus 15:20 which gives reference to Miriam the prophetess, the sister of Aaron, Deborah- Judges 4:4; Huldah- II Kings 22, the four daughters of Phillip in Acts 21:9; and Anna the prophetess in Luke 2:36 proves that God is no respecter of person and there is no concern for gender. Although the prophetess is not named in the five-fold ministry it does not mean that this gift is not important. The scriptures alone let us see that this is an prophetic gift and these woman were used and called by God. The call of these prophets/prophetess was a call to ethics, monotheism, love, righteousness, truth, goodness, justice, mercy, forbearance, and responsibility. These women were not excluded from the prophetic office in the New Testament, and were honored with the right of prophetic utterance in the New Testament.

Biblical characteristics and ministry of a prophet/prophetess can be found in the following text of scriptures: Acts 11:27-28; 13:1; 15:32; 21:10-11: I Corinthians 14:29: Ephesians 2:20; 3:3-5; 4:11-12; Exodus 15:20; Judges 4:4; and Acts 21:9.

Evangelist – (Greek words: evangelizo, "evangelion" evangelist) these are relevant Greek words used in different context of scriptures where as evangelize is used 55 times, evangelion 77 times and evangelists used only 3 times. The root word of "evangelist" which is the Greek word for "gospel" is used 85 times in the New Testament. In the King James Version Bible the verb evangelize is translated "preach", preach the gospel; "bring good tiding" and "declared". It is to bring someone into relation with the divine glad message of **salvation.** Jesus is the first "**evangelist** "of the New Testament. He went preaching the "good news" (Matthew 4:23). Although every Christian believer is commanded to proclaim the "good news" which is called evangelism many choose not to do so. Some are not called to the five-fold ascension gifts as an evangelist, but all Christian believers are called to share the gospel of Jesus Christ.

In Greek (eu means "good" and angelos translated nearly always "angel" means messenger) an evangelist is one who is sent in order to announce, teach, or perform anything. The evangelist ascension gift is one who speaks the truth in love and confidence that the gospel message will bring deliverance. Evangelist in some churches is one that travels from town to town and from church to church spreading the gospel of Jesus (Acts 8:4). They are not just an itinerant preacher merely going from place to place preaching for what he/she can get in special contributions. Also not one who only holds gospel meetings or "revivals". An evangelist is a "minister" who executes the commands of one another, bringer or bearer of good tidings; preacher of the gospel; they are flexible because when one door closes **God** opens another.

The evangelist needs full knowledge and understanding of the gospel to do his/her work for the "kingdom" of God. They must preach the word of God, be able to face anyone with truth, correct opponents of the truth, and proclaim the scriptures for the reason that they alone are profitable for the things necessary for one's spiritual growth and maturity. They are not to preach his/her opinion but the whole counsel of revealed truth. Here are some scriptures that will help you take a closer look of how an evangelist is another connection to the five-fold ascension gifts: Matthew 28:18-20; Ii Timothy 4:1-4; Romans 1:6; II Timothy 2:25; II Timothy 3:16; Acts 20:27; I Timothy 4:14; II Timothy 4:5, and Ephesians 4:11. The only person in the New Testament who is called an **evangelist** is Phillip (Acts 21:8) who is also the father of the four **daughters with the prophetic gifts.** There are many well know evangelist today who have paved the way by the leading of the Holy Spirit so that the gospel of Jesus Christ can be shared to reach many that are lost. **Salvation** is available to all! **Now Is the Time!**

An evangelist does not "rest on his/her laurels", but take advantage of spiritual momentum and keeps preaching wherever he or she goes. An evangelist knows that people in a seemingly hopeless situation can be set free when the gospel is preached to them. Matthew 11:5 states: the blind receive their sight and the lame walk, the lepers are cleansed, and the deaf hear, the dead raised up, and the poor have the gospel preached to them. They can live without fear (Luke 2:10). They may develop a strategic plan to share the word in there area knowing that nothing will stop those who hunger for truth from receiving it. An evangelist does not let persecution deter them from preaching the Gospel. The message brings peace to those who believe it. The resurrection of Jesus Christ is a part of the good news and is what many evangelists go out proclaiming and declaring for the kingdom.

They are not ashamed of the gospel of Jesus Christ for it is the power of God unto salvation to everyone that believes (Romans 1:16). The power of the gospel is what frees us from being ashamed of the gospel. The power of the gospel is to bring about salvation and deliverance which sets us free. Jesus triumphed over shame by looking at the future joy that was set before him as He died on the cross. You don't have to be ashamed of the gospel because it doesn't just make converts it saves converts. This is what makes us bold with the gospel, not that it can only make converts because any religion can do that, but it is the only one truth in the world that can really save people forever and bring them to everlasting joy with God (Romans 10:9; John 3:16-17). Remember we have a relationship with Jesus Christ not a religion. Reference Scriptures: II Thessalonians 2:13; II Corinthians 7:10; Hebrews 9:8; I Peter 1:5; Romans 5:9-10; Romans 13:11; Romans 8:32.

An evangelist not only win the lost, they also "fires up" believers to go and win the lost. Romans 10:14 clearly is an example in scripture how an evangelist longs for others to believe the Good News about Jesus Christ and realize that he/she is one who is called to "go stand and tell the people about the full message of the new life". The prophecy from Isaiah 61 is very significant that Jesus read in the synagogue in Nazareth near the beginning of His ministry speaks first of His evangelism (Luke 4:18-19).

"The spirit of the Lord is upon me because he hath anointed me to preach the gospel (evangelizo) to the poor; he has sent me to heal the brokenhearted, to preach deliverance to the captive, and recovering of sight to the blind, to set at liberty them that are bruised, to preach the acceptable year of the Lord".

Pastor – (Greek word: poimen) means herdsmen, a shepherd one who cares for, feed, guides, and protects the sheep, The greek word poimen is translated as "shepherd" 17 times in the New Testament, below are its various uses; 4 times it is used of literal shepherds caring for literal sheep; 8 times it refers to Jesus as the Great Shepherd of the church, 4 times it refers to leadership of true believers, as either true or false leadings, and 1 time it is used of an office in the church. The literal meaning of the word poimen is shepherd. English translation of the Bible only translate poimen as "pastor' only one time in the entire New testament in Ephesians 4:11; And he gave some apostles, and some prophets, and some evangelists, and some pastors and teachers (NAS). Here pastors is listed as one of the God appointed offices in the church, but it is plural ("pastors") and rules of Greek grammar here demand that pastors are teachers, refers to one office.

This gift is the only dual gift in the New Testament. There are no two gifts here. It is one gift which has two distinct dimensions. The two belong together no one can be a Pastor if he can't teach, because the teacher needs the knowledge which pastoral experience gives. So if we accurately translate poimen to be shepherds and it is one office, more properly Ephesians 4:11 reads "shepherds as teachers". In all contexts, other than Ephesians 4:11, poimen is used as shepherd because God's people are viewed as sheep of the flock. It is obvious that the contemporary Bible translators used their rendering of poimen as pastors in Ephesians 4:11. Below are scriptures other than Ephesians 4:11 where poimen is used:

Matthew 9:36	Luke 2:8	John 10:4
Matthew 26:31	Luke 2:15	John10:11
Mark 6:34	Luke 2:18	Hebrews 13:20
Mark 14:27	Luke 2:20	I Peter 2:25
John10:2		

In John 10:11 Jesus gives this term as a name for Himself "I am the Good Shepherd". He tells us Christ is the Great Shepherd of the church, the husband is the shepherd of his wife, and likewise, the pastor is the shepherd of his "flocks", the church. The last two ascension gifts mentioned by Paul are "pastors and teachers". If you were to read through the pages of the New Testament, you will not find any of the church leaders called "pastors", you would locate those given the titles of apostles, elders, overseers, and deacons but no one called "pastors".

The word pastor to most believers is associated with shepherd. The most obvious way to understand the role of the "pastor" ministry is to describe what they should do such as equipping the saints for service, building up the body of Christ, establishing unity, imparting knowledge of Jesus Christ which is the word of God, helping Christians to become mature, binding the body together, and to ensure that new believers are discipled. It is important to recognize that the role of pastors was not peculiar in the New Testament church of God. God clearly expects a lot of his pastors but he doesn't leave them to do it on their own, in their own strength and suffering (Philippians 4:13; II Corinthians 3:4-6 KJV). In Jeremiah God gives us a wonderful prophecy,. Jeremiah 3:15 says: "I will give you shepherds according to my heart, who will feed you with knowledge (of God) an understanding (of His way)". God had high expectations, even back then of His pastors and He upbraided them when they did not fulfill those expectations. As the mouth piece of God Jeremiah declares "For the shepherds (of the people) have been like brutes: irrational and stupid, and have not sought the Lord or inquired Him (by necessity and by right of His word). Therefore they have not dealt prudently and have not prospered, and all their flocks are scattered" (Jeremiah 10:21 Amplified Bible).

In Titus 1:9 the scripture reads that the pastor must be one "holding fast the faithful word as he hath been taught, that he may be able by sound doctrine both to exhort and to convince the gainsavers." Peter also emphasized this by exhorting "Feed the flock of God which is among you" (I Peter 5:2). When Jesus was recommissioning Peter after the resurrection, twice He used the word boshe meaning specifically to nourish or provide food, "Feed my lambs" (John 21:15) pastors and teachers (NAS). This is most obvious to the preaching and teaching ministry of the Pastor. God expects His pastors and His shepherds to spiritually feed (that is nourish) God's people. In the New

Testament section of the Bible, you see yet further clarification of the pastor's role in ministry. The letter to the Hebrews ends with an exhortation to the church about the believer's attitude toward the pastor and with it you get further insight into what a pastor has to be engaged in.

Paul writes;

> "obey those who rule over you, and be submissive, for they watch out for your souls,
> as those who must give account ." (Hebrews 13:17 NKJV)

So from this we see the pastor who is the overseer of the flock -must watch out for his members souls. This is bound to involve at times exhorting against sin. Exhortation usually involves correction, a call to dispense with the bad or less than best in order to take hold of God's best for you. Correction isn't easy to take but it's necessary. Those who accept it and are improved by it will receive a good reward (Hebrews 12:11). God's job description of the office of Pastor as we have seen through scripture sets well boundaries of his duties. In a given church situation the pastor may have to take on other roles beside that of pastor. He may face challenges to maintain the effectiveness of his Pastoral roles but he can face them with the power of the Holy Spirit. In closing, let us carefully take to heart the words of Ezekiel the prophet, who warns the shepherd of Yahweh's judgment if ever they use force and severity to dominate the flock. (Ezekiel 34:1-4; 7-20; 23-24; 29-31) NKJV

Teacher – (Greek word: didasko) which is the product of didaskalos "to teach or to give instructions". As we see in scripture of Matthew 28:18-20: And Jesus came and spake unto them, saying *"All power is given unto me in heaven and in earth. Go ye therefore and teach all nations, baptizing them in the name of the Father, and of the Son, and of the Holy Spirit. Teaching them to observe all things whatsoever I have commanded you: and lo, I am with you always, even unto the end of the world.* Amen. Jesus has given a command to teach while in Matthew 4:23 says: "Jesus about all Galilee teaching (didasko) in their synagogues". Jesus who was a teacher also ministered to the people by teaching them. It was apart of His ministry. The teacher therefore, walks in his ministry, where Jesus walked. The person who stands in the office of a teacher, will be able to explain spiritual truth in such a way that is easily understood. It is not learned by human effort, but is by the anointing of the Holy Spirit. In I Corinthians 2:12-13 Paul said, no man teaches me but the Holy Spirit. The teaching office, is an office (Ephesians 4:11-12) and the office of the teacher is needed in the church, to root and ground people in the word of God (Psalm 1:1-3 KJV).

Some people can have natural ability or desire to teach but that does not qualify them to stand in the office of a teacher. The Holy Spirit gave sets in the church, and anoints the one that He chooses. The anointing is the ability of God, working through mortal man. The teacher him/herself is always teachable. Even before Saul was converted he sat at the feet of Gamaliel and was taught, which later he continued to spend time in school preparing for the New Testament truths (Galatians 2:15-18). Paul the teacher was a student to the very end of his kingdom assignment (II Timothy

4:13). Teachers are always prepared because of their diligent study of God's word and seeking Him. The function of this gift was to thoroughly instruct young believers "to observe all things" Christ has commanded. Acts 2:42 reads; "And they continued steadfastly in the apostle doctrine and fellowship, and in breaking of bread and in prayers". The teaching ministry can be exercised in a home, bible study, Sunday school classes, or even Christian Colleges and Universities.

I have personally experienced the gift of teaching both in the kingdom system and the secular system. I've taught many through this gift from all walks of life, young and old. God has allowed me to use my gift under the anointing of the Holy Spirit. The ministry of teaching the Word to my children in our home, teaching children/youth in Sunday school, and also adult classes at church has truly been a gift from God. Teaching in both roles has always required preparation and diligence in what God equipped me to do. This gift requires patience, love, and commitment. I could do nothing without the help of the Holy Spirit. Whether it's in the kingdom system or the secular (educational) system the gift is being used. The teaching gift enables the person endowed to as readily present more difficult truth (Hebrews 5:10) to those who are able to receive it. Teaching the students or (congregation) regardless of what levels it is important because it helps the students to grow just as well as the church to grow. Always, remember the teaching gift involves the true Word of God so the church can be edified for the perfecting of the saints.

Here are some scriptures that give us insight on the role of the teaching ministry: I Corinthians 3:1-2; Hebrews 5:12-14; and I Peter 2:2.

Regardless of what ascension gift is exercised it's from Christ. It also requires lots of work and love for the work. The role of the teacher is vital because of the spiritual and doctrinal functions of the church. The church depends upon them and the teachers are the ones who do the ground work. Throughout the gospels, we find the Lord standing in the teaching office, conveying spiritual truth by using simple (parables), ordinary everyday things. Jesus is the believer's example of the teaching office in operation Mark 4:2 says: "And he taught them many things by parables, and said unto them in his doctrine". Apostles, Prophets, Evangelists, and Teachers have been teaching God's people for many hundreds of years. Many have fulfilled the purpose and the function of these gifts which scriptures have revealed to us. They could care less about credentials conferred upon them, having printed business cards, corporate stationary, or a multicolored brochure.

The Bible teaches that every Christian has one or more gifts. Ephesians 4:7-8 says: "But to each one of us grace was given according to the measure of Christ's gift. Therefore it says when He ascended on high He led captive a head of captives, and he gave gifts to men. Spiritual gifts are listed in three principle New Testament passages found in Romans 12:4-8, I Corinthians 12:8-11,28 and Ephesians 4:11.

All Christians manifest many of these ministries in limited ways, but concentration and exceptional ability for a particular one is a "gift". The listing according to passages is as followed below:

Romans 12:4-8	I Corinthians 12:8-11, 28	Ephesians 4:11
1. Prophecy	1. Wisdom	1. Apostles
2. Ministry	2. Knowledge	2. Prophets
3. Teaching	3. Faith	3. Evangelists
4. Exhortation	4. Healing	4. Pastors
5. Giving	5. Miracles	5. Teachers
6. Leadership	6. Prophecy	
7. Mercy	7. Discerning of spirits	
	8. Tongues	
	9. Interpretation of tongues	
	10. Apostles	
	11. Teacher	
	12. Helps	
	13. Administrations	

Gifts are given and received in various ways. The spiritual gifts God gives to every believer are not like those our parents gave us. God's gifts are complete. Not only does God give to each of us spiritual gifts by which the body of Christ is supported and sustained. He also gives us all that is needed to carry out those functions vital to the spiritual health and nourishment and ministry of His body, the church. With those gifts, God gives to each of us not only a measure of grace to empower us for service He also gives a measure of faith as well.

As a result, when teaching God's Word we are no longer to be children, tossed here and there by waves, and carried about by every wind of doctrine, by the trickery of men, by craftiness in deceitful scheming; but speaking the truth in love. We are to grow up in all aspects into Him, who is the head, even Christ, from whom the whole body, being fitted and held together by that which every joint supplies, according to the proper working of each individual part, causes the growth of the body for the building up of itself in love (Ephesians 4:7-16).

We must remember all "five-fold" ascension gift ministries have faced challenges from the Old Testament Book to the New Testament Book. Many in the bible who have walked in these gifts have encountered some forms of testing, trials, pain, rejection, and other spiritual battles. Jesus faced challenges in His ministry and rejection by His family and those in His own hometown of Nazareth. He faced many who were against him including those who were His enemies. Believers will face challenges as they obediently serve God. Even today in the 21st Century many face these same or more challenges than ever before whether it is from within the church or the outside world. Christian believers who have been called to the "five-fold ascension gifts" will never ever face any challenges which can be compared to Jesus.

Some challenges could have been by these individuals' mistakes whether it was in governing or guiding. Christian believers must realize that anyone who's been called to these five-fold ascension gifts is still human and fallible, they may make wrong decisions and have incorrect personal opinions sometimes through their human characteristics, do not negate the validity of their calling. Look to the Lord for guidance. Wait upon Him! and let him guide you as you continue going forward to be used for the kingdom of God. This is especially crucial for the future existence of the church because it is only through converts that new disciples come forth. Nobody today has authority from God to lay a new foundation. The foundation of Jesus Christ has been laid by obedient Apostles, and Prophets of a previous time. True Apostles, Prophets, Evangelists, Pastors, and Teachers today only have one option: to build upon the foundation of Jesus Christ, by teaching Jesus.

This chapter gives a clear picture and understanding about the "five-fold ascension gifts" and there roles in the body of Christ. The gifts are very crucial in this season and seasons to come along with help from other gifts in the body. These five-fold ascension gifts must be used in its rightful role to effectively bring forth the kingdom of God by the power of the Holy Spirit. These are Christ "ascension gifts" given to the body of Christ to be used just as the scriptures referred to in Ephesians 4:8; 11-13 (KJV).

Chapter 3 Questions and Exercise

1. From your reading and study of this chapter why is it so important for these "five fold ascension gifts" to be used correctly in the body of Christ?

2. Look at the hand illustration in this chapter and close your book. Can you name what each gift represent in the five-fold ministries? Name the role/function of each gift?

3. Where in scripture are these five-fold gifts found in the New Testament?

4. Are these five-fold gifts working effectively in the body of Christ today?

5. Did Jesus carry any of these gifts? Do you know your spiritual gift/gifts? Are you called to the five-fold ministry? If the answer is yes, what is the gift or gifts? Are you using your gift or gifts to effectively bring forth the "kingdom of God"?

6. Although the "five-fold ascension gifts" are "kingdom connecters" to each other can you list other spiritual gifts from the New Testament?

7. Name at least three individuals in the bible who were called to each five-fold ascension gifts.

8. List the five indicators in the calling of an ascension gift or five-fold ministries in this chapter?

9. Ephesians 4:11 says: And he gave some, _____, and some, _____, and some, _____, and some, _____, and_____.

10. Paul teaches us in Ephesians 4:12 that these gifts are for the perfecting of the saints, for the _____ of the _____, for the _____of the body of Christ.

"Ask Jesus to save you now and have eternal life." Dear Lord Jesus I repent of my sins; Come into my heart and save me. I believe Romans 10:9 which says: That if thou shalt confess with thy mouth the <u>Lord Jesus,</u> and shalt believe in thine heart that God hath raised him from the dead, thou <u>shalt be saved</u>. For whosoever call upon the name of the <u>Lord shall be saved</u> (Romans 10:13).

CHAPTER 4

Kingdom Carrier

Before I formed thee in the belly I knew thee; and before thou camest forth out of the womb I sanctified thee, and I ordained thee a prophet unto the nations.
Jeremiah 1:5

From the beginning to the end God has allowed us to witness and study His word. There have been many kingdom carriers from Genesis to Revelation. They have been mentioned in the Books of the Law, History, Minor and Major Prophets, the Gospels and the Epistles. As you read this chapter you will be able to understand the importance of what you are carrying for the kingdom of God.

Are you a Kingdom Carrier? Before you can identify if you are a kingdom carrier you must first ask yourself are you apart of the kingdom? Are you really saved? The bible tells us in John 14:6: "Jesus saith unto him, *I am the way, the truth, and the life; no man cometh unto the Father but by me*". There is only one way into the kingdom and that is through Jesus Christ. John 3:16-17 declares: *For God so loved the world, that he gave his only begotten Son, that whosoever believeth in him should not perish, but have everlasting life. For God sent not his Son into the world to condemn the world; but that the world through him might be saved.* Just as Jeremiah 1:5 teaches us God knew who you were before you entered into your mother's womb. Do you believe what God has told you? Do you know your identity?

The enemy has deceived many believers with false identities and this is because he wants to destroy your true identity. Jesus knew His identity. God created you in His image and you are called to do something in the earth realm for the "kingdom". Let's take a look at Genesis 12 when God called Abram, but he chose not to acknowledge Sarai as his wife, but as his sister. The enemy deceived Abram when he lied to Pharaoh about Sarai which caused a situation that was not necessary, if only Abram knew who he was and what he had, Abram (Abraham) would not have told her to tell everyone she was his sister. Abram afraid to tell the truth after fear had came in. Sarai (Sarah) a beautiful woman not his sister, but his wife did exactly what her husand told her to do. The blessing was what God had said not the lie that he was deceived by. Abram (identity) was more than what he saw in himself. The enemy convinced Abram in doing this because he knew Abram (Abraham) was a "kingdom carrier" of nations . When Abram (Abraham) realized who he was and what he had God used him for the kingdom purpose.

Know Who You Are

In the book of Genesis Chapter 1:26-27 the scriptures tells us God said; Let us make man in our image after our likeness: So God created man in his own image; in the image of God created he him; male and female created he them. You were created for a kingdom purpose as a carrier. A kingdom carrier is one who has totally surrendered their life to Christ which involves your spirit, mind, body, and soul. Romans 12:1-2 says your body must be presented as a living sacrifice and your mind must not be conformed to this world but renewed and transformed to the word of God. Spend time with God and practice being in His presence with worship and thanksgiving. Praying and studying the Word of God must be a priority in the carrier's life. Being able to discern and rightly divide the word of truth because so many would have us to believe what we know is right is now wrong. You are the light of the earth.

When Christ is in you, you love like Christ, live and walk like Christ in the fruit of the spirits. Your attitude and behavior changes because you are being changed. Kingdom Carriers are movers and shakers, trail blazers, some are forerunners for Jesus, and they make a difference in the world. They set the tone when they enter a room, the atmosphere must shift and accommodate to the Word of God because of their presence. They are threats to the kingdom of darkness (Satan) and Satan can't stop them from fulfilling their God ordained purpose and destiny. God has not prepared you to be defeated. God has a plan for your life. Jeremiah 29:11 clearly states: For I know the thoughts that I think toward you, saith the Lord thoughts of peace; and not of evil, to give you an expected end. They walk in authority with boldness to speak the truth in indignation and compassion when needed.

Kingdom carriers don't compromise, bargain, make a deal or water down the Word of God to appease those with itching ears. Walking in the light and not in darkness is your life style along with living by truth and righteousness because Jesus is the Light and truth (I John 1:5-10). They have the character and very nature of God which reveals the fruit of the spirits (Galatians 5:21-23 KJV). **Jesus knew His true identity.** In the gospel of John there were 7 "I AM" in scriptures revealing who Jesus was. Let's take a look at each one below:

" I AM the bread of life".........................John 6: 35
" I AM the light of the world"...............John 8:12
" I AM the door".................................John 10:7

" I AM the Good Shepherd"....................John 10:11
" I AM the resurrection and the life".........John 11:25
" I AM the way, the truth, and the life".......John 14:6
" I AM the true vine"..........................John 15:1

Kingdom carriers know who they are, wear the full armor of God, and know that they are a very powerful individual (Ephesians 6:10-19 KJV). They are not called by man, but called and chosen by God to do the work of the kingdom in order to help God's people. You must be spiritually fit to carry what God has inside of you to physically run the race that is set before you (Hebrews 12:1).

Kingdom Carriers are those who have faith to receive the invisible, believe the incredible, does the impossible, and they also walk in obedience and are willing to sacrifice. When we recount how God gave David overwhelming victory over any and every enemy that attacked him we have assurance to feel victorious just as David did. God gives us that same overwhelming victory over any and every enemy because we are kingdom carriers. Psalm 18:37-38 states: I have pursued my enemies, and over taken them; neither did I turn again till they were consumed. I have wounded them that they were not able to rise: they are fallen under my feet. We must see our spiritual enemies as they truly are –already defeated in Christ and subject to kingdom authority. There should be no compromise and no prisoners! Be ruthless against every high thought that exalt itself above the knowledge of God (II Corinthians 10:5) never wavering in your spiritual warfare against God's enemies. We must always remember to guard our spirits and brace ourselves for the deceiver. The enemy seizes to deceive more and more of God's leaders and servants in the body of Christ now more than ever (Galatians 6:7; Ephesians 5:6, KJV).

Paul states that in all these things you are more than a conqueror through Him who loved you (Romans 8:37). Declare with him, and I am convinced that nothing can separate us from his love. Death can't and life can't, nor angels, nor principalities, nor powers, nor things present, nor things to come. Nor height, nor depth, nor any other creature, shall be able to separate us from the love of God, which is in Christ Jesus our Lord (Romans 8:38-39 KJV). I beseech you my brothers and sisters go forward against your enemies, and don't stop, don't quit until the enemy has been crushed and under your feet. Remember you are a kingdom carrier! God has allowed you to go through preparation, which involves studying His word, training, times of waiting, pain, rejection, isolation, because of what you are carrying. God is still preparing many today for their kingdom assignment regardless of how different the assignment is, the time frame in waiting may not be quite as long as for someone else, but the characteristics of a kingdom carrier are still the same.

Kingdom carriers do what Jesus did. Jesus had a ministry of power. When Jesus was in the upper room He promised His followers that they would do even greater works than He. In John 14:12 Jesus speaks and says: *Verily verily, I say unto you, He that believeth on me, the works that I do shall he do also; and greater works that these shall he do: because I go unto my Father*". Doing what Jesus did in practice of personal trans-function, His practice in prayer, silence, and solitude, fasting, frugality, chastity, service, and stewardship. Jesus worked with those who followed Him. Yes they followed Jesus! Kingdom carriers know they have a covenant with God when they step in Christ. Whether related to Jesus by birth or not it's because of Jesus we are connected. We must live according to the promises of God and the covenant of that promise (Genesis 13:2, 5; 22:1-7 KJV). We are people of the kingdom.

We need to know that Satan does exist whether we here it preached or taught in the body of Christ more often or not. Satan is not a pitched fork devil running around in a red costume which is often portrayed by the worldly media. Many believers have bought into the deception thinking the lie is truth and they have no power to defeat the devil. We must study and know God's word so we are able to spiritually fight the enemy and know the resurrection power of Jesus Christ that dwells within us. I Peter 5:8 warns us and states: Be sober, be vigilant, because your adversary the devil, as a roaring lion, walketh about, seeking who he may devour.

Jesus bound the spirits of fear by speaking peace to the trouble. He stated in Matthew 14:27 *"Fear thou not! Peace be unto you! It is I!"* God has not given us the spirit of fear.

Some kingdom carriers are like palm trees, they bend but do not break. A palm tree will stand and not break in the midst of the wind, it will begin to sway while the wind is blowing, bending in every direction, but does not break in the storm. Just like the storms of life we will bend but we don't break. They are God's vessel that totally without compromise walks and live by the Word of God. They don't walk and live by the ideology of Islam, Mormons, Scientology, Buddhism, Kabala, New Age Religion, and others whose teaching contradicts the truth and authentic Word of God. Amos Chapter 3:3 says: "Can two walk together except they be agreed". Don't misunderstand what I'm saying yes, we're to share the gospel of Jesus Christ with all those who will hear, yet never ever compromise the Word of God to conform to the ideological standards of false doctrines. Jesus is the way, the truth, and the life (John 14:6).

As you continue to walk in the will of God the kingdom carrier knows the frequency of God. They can hear His voice clearly when God speaks whether it is through a still quiet voice, through His word in scripture, through His prophets/leaders, through weather patterns, and even through a disaster storm/calm winds. A Kingdom Carrier must remember they are making a great difference in the world of darkness because your standards are based on God's standards. The kingdom carrier believes the infallible, inspired word which is the absolute truth (the Word of God). You are salt and your light shines brightly before man, standing in the mist of gross darkness everywhere. God's glory shines on you! Isaiah 60:1-2 declares; Arise, shine for thy light is come, and the glory of the Lord is risen upon thee. For, behold the darkness shall cover the earth, and gross darkness the people; but the Lord shall arise upon thee; and his glory shall be seen upon thee. (KJV)

Knowing who you are and who you belong to is vital to your Christian walk. Christians are not just about trends and traditions of this world. Our salt and light is different from the world and its cultures. We don't try to fit in the world's way; the world has to fit in our way. The church should always be the one that the world can see the difference but today many Christians are so busy trying to fit in with the world that they look like them instead of them becoming to look like us. Know who you are! In John 17:14-16 Jesus clearly speaks and tells us "we are not of the world, even as He is not of the world". (KJV)

Know Who Is In You

Do you believe that Christ is in you? If you believe that Christ is in you, when was the last time you thanked God for Him? Colossians 1:27 states: To whom God would make known what is the riches of the glory of this mystery among the Gentiles; which is Christ in you the hope of glory. A mystery is a truth undiscovered, except by revelation. In scripture a mystery maybe in fact which, when revealed we cannot understand in details, though we know it and act upon it. Christ is present in my inner life. Know who is in you! You don't have to ascend to heaven to find Him, nor descend into the depths to bring Him, neither do you have to go on a long journey to reach Him. Jesus Christ has given you himself because you do not have what it takes to live the Christian life.

When you know who is in you (Christ) there is a hope of displaying His nature and character. There is a hope of being with the Lord in heaven one day. Our hope then is not in ourselves, but in Christ. In our own strength we fall, but through dependence upon Christ we stand because he dwells in us .We can now break free from the bondage of sin. Exodus 33:12-14 states: "And Moses said unto the Lord, see thou sayest unto me, Bring up this people: and thou hast not let me know who thou wilt send with me. Yet thou hast said, I know thee by name, and thou hast also found grace in thy sight, show me now thy way, that I may find grace in thy sight: and consider that this nation is thy people. And he said, "My presence shall go with thee, and I will give thee rest". Clearly we can see from this text that Moses needed to ask God this question.

Praying in the spirit should be a part of your daily regimen because of Christ who lives in you. Jude 1:20 says: But ye, beloved, building up yourselves on your most holy faith, praying in the Holy Ghost. There is a time to speak in our heavenly language (tongues), and a time for declaration. Job 22:28 says: "Thou shalt also decree a thing and it shall be established unto thee; and the light shall shine upon thy ways". The declaration proceeds the manifestation. Conceive it! See it! Believe it! Expect it! Psalm 33:8-9 also states: Let all the earth fear the Lord; let all the inhabitation of the world stand in awe of him, For he spake and it was done; he commanded, and it stood fast. As a Christian believer you just can't do anything you want, hang with any and everybody, go in any old environment, and places any more. Remember you are the called out ones. Only the Holy Spirit can lead you to the places and environment you should be in because God can use you as an effective witness to un-believers by His word or your life style.

Romans 5:2-4 says: "And we rejoice in the hope of the glory of God. Not only so, but we also rejoice in our suffering, because we know that suffering produces perseverance, perseverance produces character, and character produces hope. Perseverance is the key to every great accomplishment because nothing of lasting value has ever been achieved without it. When you start a thing, don't quit until you finish it. What ever God has called and chosen you to do don't quit because Christ the "hope of glory" lives in you.

The path ahead of you can sometimes be filled with obstacles, people will oppose you, but yet you should be determined to persevere. There will be financial setbacks, time pressures, illness, and misfortunes but some of the biggest obstacles will come from inside of you. Don't question when trouble hits and whine or complain about it. You are anointed, you're powerful, and a threat to Satan's kingdom. The enemy comes in to bring you doubt, hopelessness, and despair but Jesus Christ the "hope of glory" lives in you. Let the Lord allow you to stand with perseverance as you continue the journey toward your kingdom assignments. There may be a sense of self doubt-insecurity, procrastination, and worry but you must give yourself permission to succeed because of Christ who is in you. When we persevere through adversity we win the approval of our Lord Jesus Christ, who told the suffering church at Ephesus, "I know your deeds, your hard work and your perseverance...you have persevered and have endured hardship for my name, and have not grown weary" (Revelation 2:1-3). I'm sure this is the commendation Joseph received from God when he passed the perseverance test.

Perseverance is a refusal to quit. We need to remember that perseverance is not a matter of forcing doors to open; it's standing in front of the doors as long as it takes before God chooses to open them. Life is a marathon not a sprint. The race doesn't go to the swiftest, but to those who don't give up (Ecclesiastes 9:11). We need endurance in order to deal with the burden of adversity. We must maintain a balanced spiritual diet, exercise regularly, and get plenty of rest. People give up or get out when they feel depleted-when they physically, emotionally, and spiritually run out of gas yet Christ in you through the power of the Holy Spirit will strengthen you. When going through adversity, watch out for pessimists, blamers, and toxic personalities. Beware of people who try to talk you out of your dreams and goals. Seek out people of faith. Persevere to the end!

A Christian believer must do all they can to live for Christ. Some believe that the more committed, consecrated, giving tithes regularly, working in ministries/volunteering, and self-sacrificing they are the greatest Christian they can become. They feel some sense of acceptance and favor with God and their peers. There is one problem with this belief and thinking. No one can live the Christian life without Christ and the power of the Holy Spirit in you. The indwelling presence of Jesus in the human "heart" is the manifestation of the eternal mystery (hope of glory). It is not accomplished by our living for Christ, but by Christ living His life through us. This is called the "exchanged life" or "crucified life" that is stated in (Galatians 2:20 and Romans 6:6 KJV). God is reaching down to man, while religion is reaching up to God. Colossians 3:4 clearly states: When

Christ who is our life, shall appear, then shall ye also appear with him in glory. Christ is our life and the truth. Christian life is Christ living His life through us.

Cross References: Matthew 13:11; Romans 8:10; Ephesians 1:7; Ephesians 1:18; Ephesians 3:16; and I Timothy 1:16.

Know Your Gift

Do you know your gift(s) that God has placed in you? Have you ever asked yourself what are your gifts? Paul clearly states in Romans 11:29, "For the gifts and calling of God are without repentance". God gave the gifts to us because He desired them to be used. Our gifts and talents are to be used for the glory of God. Don't let anyone pervert your gift (s).We can't allow others to manipulate or tell us what gifts we have or don't have and dictate what God wants to do with the gifts and talents that are in us. Don't let man's rejection or player haters influence you or stop you from moving forward. Let rejection propel you to get closer with God and the player haters push you more toward your destiny. You know who you are, hold on God is not through with you and you will use your gifts for the glory of God.

Man has created the obstacles, God never forbade us from using our gifts and talents. I Peter 1:16 says: "Be ye holy for I am holy" (KJV). God said "**sin not**". Man decided that being holy should move below the scriptural parameter, and began setting boundaries which fit their definition of holiness. Jesus said, *"I have come that they may have life, and that they may have it more abundantly"* (John 10:10 NKJV). Man tells us what we can do. Denominational rules, standards and regulations have caused the church to compare gifts/talents and compete with one another. This has caused the church to exchange one form of religiosity for another. God wants you to use your gift (s)! Your job is not your work (skills)! Yes! we all may have skills but your gift is more important than your skills. If your job is more important than your gift, there's the problem. The calling/ministry you were born to do (gifts) can be used while you are on the job (Jeremiah 1:5 KJV). We must use our gifts in the body of Christ just as well as in the world.

Get up off the pew/chair! Don't just warm a pew/chair on Sunday's! Is your life counting for Jesus? Are you impacting anyone by your life? Have you led someone to Christ, or offered an encouraging word in the name of Jesus. As James writes "Every good gift and every perfect gift is from above, and comes down from the Father of lights, with whom there is no variation neither shadow of turning" (James 1:17 NKJV). There is a purpose for your gift(s) in the body of Christ. God can use your gift(s) when and where ever He chooses. Every gift(s) are important to God and you should feel the same way.

There are many biblical scriptures which refer to "gift" or "gifts" such as Proverbs 18:16 says: "A man's gift maketh room for him and bringeth him before great men". I Timothy 4:14 says: "Neglect not the gift that is in thee, which was given thee by prophecy, with the laying on of hands of the presbytery. II Timothy 1:6 says: "Wherefore I put thee in remembrance that thou stir up the gift of God, which is in thee by the putting on of my hands and Romans 1:11 states, "For I long to see you that I may impart unto you some spiritual gift, to the end ye may be established". Paul even shared this in I Corinthians Chapter 12 as he talks about the spiritual gifts. God has bestowed on us which there are diversities of operations but it is the same God which worketh all in all. I Corinthians Chapter 12:4 says: "Now there are diversities of gifts but the same Spirit". Many believers have often seemed to astonishingly base their walk with God on the gift(s) they possess. Paul writes in I Corinthians 13:1-4 regardless of what gifts we have if we don't have charity (love) we are nothing. Of the three gifts mentioned in I Corinthians Chapter 13:13 states: And now abideth faith, hope, charity, these three; but the greatest of these is charity. In I Corinthians Chapter 12:31 the "best gifts" mentioned here refer to those which are most useful. The Corinthian believers were desiring the gifts that would bring them the most acclaim and prestige among their fellow brethren in Christ (the gifts of tongues, prophecies, and knowledge, cf. I Corinthians 13:8). Instead Paul urged, them to "covet" (earnestly desire) the gifts that would best benefit the cause of Christ, not themselves in Chapter 13. Paul further explains that spiritual gifts must be done in love for Christ, not for self. Although God has given you gift(s) never ever forget that we could do nothing without God and the power of the Holy Spirit. Know the gift(s) in you!

Know Your Authority

Do you know as a child of God's kingdom you have authority and power to defeat the devil (enemy). Jesus knew His authority and was a man of authority. As Christian believers we have authority but we are also subject to authority. Many of us are using our gifts on jobs where we are in authority over others and in others cases someone has authority over us. Knowing when to use that authority can be very difficult or challenging at times. I personally have experience with both sides of the coin where as those in charge have had authority over me, and where as I'm now in a position of authority over others. I faced spiritual warfare and resistance from those who I supervise literally on a daily basis. The spiritual warfare comes from believers and un-believers alike. Many of my experiences have been spiritual battles coming from those who say they are walking with Christ contrary to the fact they raise more hell than the un-believer (sinner).

Whatever position you find yourself in beware of your surroundings and always have your spiritual antennas up so you are able to discern the spirits around you so you know how and when to use your God given authority. Through personal experiences I have witnessed Christians who want to show off their authority just because they could. These individuals talk the Word but really aren't saying anything. Some of them compromises what's right and follow the masses (world) conforming to what is wrong just to appease those in their close circle. Be not deceived when their playing Christian music, has a bible on their desk, quoting and misquoting scriptures because truly there should be some type of change when you're walking in the authority of Jesus Christ. One in authority doesn't have to say anything unless it's necessary to do so depending on the circumstances. There are many leaders in authority in the church that are all about fluff, no substance, and their mind-set is based on having a form of godliness but denying the power thereof (II Timothy 3:5 KJV).

Jesus even warns us of those which comes in sheep clothing but inwardly they are ravening wolves. In Matthew Chapter 7:21-23 Jesus clearly states: *"Not every one that saith unto me; Lord, Lord shall enter into the kingdom of heaven, but he that doeth the will of my Father which is in heaven. Many will say to me that day; Lord, Lord have we not prophesied in thy name? And in thy name have we not cast out devils? And in thy name done many wonderful works? And then will I profess unto them, I never knew you; depart from me, ye that work iniquity.* (KJV)

Challenges are faced in the body of Christ because those in authority think they are better, more intelligent, more important, and believe they have earned the right to speak and say what ever they choose to God's people. Many have used and abused their God given authority regardless of where, when, and how it's impacted others. Many church leaders in authority have used that same authority to reject, criticize, hold back, keep down, and put a blanket on those whom God has called with an anointing/power to do kingdom business in the body of Christ, but was not allowed to do based on man's standards, lack of discernment, position of power, and man made rules. Remember God is always in control yet He allowed this to happen even when it's under handed by man. There have been many Christian believers whom have left the church because of how they've seen the way many individuals used their authority.

In the kingdom your authority is not based on the many degrees, accolades, Emmy's, Grammy's, or Dove awards. Yes! you have all these things and now what? Are you really satisfied? Do you honestly believe that Jesus wants you to bring all this in the kingdom? This is just another twisted mind-set of mankind. Many believers have fallen to believe that more and more is better missing the whole concept of why Jesus came and what the purpose of the kingdom message is all about. God has not given us the authority to hurt, crush, wound, neglect, and condemn others in the body of Christ or the world. Jesus came to **save** that which was lost not to condemn. There has not been any remorse or repentance by some leaders in authority or church members in the body of Christ on how they have hurt, neglected, and wounded others in the house of God in which they may have come in contact with. They believe this is okay! They fit right in with the world.

Although many have authority whether its kingdom or of the world there is a huge difference. The kingdom authority is with power from God, as the authority from man is like dust in the wind, it comes and goes. Now you see it and now you don't! Jesus knew who He was and had all authority with power. Jesus didn't go around bragging who He was and what authority He carried. He didn't have to say anything when He entered a room, His very presence spoke volumes. Who's authority are you walking in and following? Jesus acknowledges that he could do nothing of himself but the will of the Father who sent him. Jesus said unto them, *"My meat is to do the will of him that sent me, and to finish his work"* (John 4:34). God has given you authority where ever you are, whether its in your home, on your job, church, your business, organizations, or group activities, but how and when you use that authority must be pleasing to God.

When ever we face a situation, challenge, or problems just ask ourselves "What Would Jesus Do? Even the centurion man had faith to believe, and knew Jesus was a man of authority and had the power to heal his servant. Matthew Chapter 8:7-10 says: "And Jesus saith unto him,*" I will come and heal him".* The centurion answered and said, LORD I am not worthy that thou shouldest come under my roof; but speak the word only, and my servant shall be healed. For I am a man under authority, having soliders under me; and I say to this man, Go; and he goeth; and to another, come and he cometh; and to my servant, Do this, and he doeth it. When Jesus heard it, he marveled, and said to them that followed, *verily I say unto you, I have not found so great faith, no not in Israel.* (KJV)

As Christian believers we must use the authority that God has given us to benefit the kingdom and bring glory to His name.

Know Your Power

Do you know that God has given you power through Jesus Christ. For in Him we live, and move, and have our being, as also some of your own poets have said, For we are also His offspring, the scriptures clearly states in Acts 17:28 and Philippians 3:10 says: that I may know Him, and the power of His resurrection, and the fellowship of His sufferings, being made conformable unto His death (KJV). When Jesus Christ died on the cross and shed His blood for your sins and mine He rose from the dead with resurrection power. We have that same power today because of the blood of Jesus. The **blood speaks**! Luke Chapter 10:19 in fact gives us and understanding about our power. In fact the scripture states: "Behold I give you power to tread on serpents and scorpions, and over all the power of the enemy: and nothing shall by any means hurt you"!

Know the power you carry! Be not afraid of Satan (enemy, devil, thief) and yes he came to steal, kill, and destroy you (us). Jesus said; *"The thief cometh not, but for to steal, and to kill and to destroy: I am come that thy might have life, and that they might have it more abundantly"* (John 10:10 KJV). The Lord even warns Peter and said, *Simon, Simon behold Satan hath desires to have you, that he may sift you as wheat; But I prayed for thee' that thy faith fail not: and when thou are converted, strengthen thy brethren* (Luke 22:31-32 KJV).

In Acts 26:18 the Greek word for "power" here is "exousia" which means "ability, privilege, mastery, influence" and denoted "freedom of action, the right to act" when used of God, it is absolute; unrestricted, "authority, ability, force, strength". In other words, the word "exousia" is "ability" while the word "dunamis" is better translated "dynamic" power in the sense that we normally think of truly dynamic power. In this text of scripture "from the power of Satan unto God" means that you should turn from the "ability" of Satan to the ability of God.

The devil has no power over you (us). Fear and deceit is two of Satan's weapons he often uses against Christian believers. Even the deception that is here now in the earth realm is used to look real when it's not. Many things look bad, things look worse, and deception is getting you to speak things that are contrary to God's will for you and His word. Speak the Word with power that resides in you. Remember, Satan is a liar and deceiver. Be not deceived; God will never deceive us (Numbers 23:19 KJV). The only thing Satan has is the ability to bring fear and deception to you. There are lots of people that consider Satan to be an all-powerful being, when in fact he is not. He lost whatever power he had as an anointed cherub of God when he was cast out of heaven and fell to earth (Luke 10:18).

When we look at Isaiah 14:12-14 Satan (Lucifer) is not equal to God in any way, and he never was. We have to realize that he is a disenfranchised spirit that is seeking those he might deceive. I Peter 5:8 says: Be sober, be vigilant; because your adversary the devil, as a roaring lion, walketh about, seeking whom he may devour. Satan does use fear and doubt and your own authority/power against you by getting you to say things that are out of line with God's word. This is the clever way he uses fear and doubt to keep things off track with the thoughts that may seduce and influence what power you have or not which is Satan's plan in your life. Remember God has given you (us) faith to move mountains, but faith without works is useless. Faith is seeking something done in the spiritual realm, and not just seeking it, but believing it (Hebrews 11:1 KJV).

When we have the power and authority given to us by the Creator of the universe, then we have the power and authority to stomp over the snake that is definitely under our feet. The kingdom power and authority is available to us today. Paul, by the Spirit of God stated: "For the kingdom of God is not in word but in power (I Corinthians 4:20). He is saying the kingdom of God is not just words with power but God's kingdom is a kingdom of power. All power is given to the King of this Kingdom, Jesus Christ (Anointed One) as Ruler of all that existed, all there is and ever will be. He has all power in Himself. He gives His power to His followers and we represent Him on this earth today and forever. Jesus the one who is power spoke peace to the spirits of fear, healed the sick and diseased, cast out demons, performed many miracles, and even raised the dead. Remember you have the power to do the same.

As Kingdom Carriers you daily continue to transform to a kingdom mind-set in which the gospel will develop the person of Christ in you, the book of Acts develops the work of Christ in you, and the Epistles develops the doctrine of Christ in you. This chapter is to help you know your true identity in Christ, who's you are, your gift(s), your authority and the power you carry. Jesus Christ is the ultimate and only perfect kingdom carrier who was about His Fathers business on His kingdom assignment to **save** the world. Jesus Christ is the kingdom!!!

Protecting the Seed

A kingdom carrier is very protective of what comes in and around their spirit; they nourish what God has given them by eating spiritual (reading the word) and healthy foods. The bible says in Deuteronomy 8:3, "And he humbled thee, and suffered thee to hunger, and fed thee with manna, which thou knewest not, neither did thy fathers know; that he might make thee know that man doth not live by bread only, but by every *word* that proceedeth out of the mouth of the Lord doth man, live." The word that God has in you is quick, and powerful, and sharper than any two-edged sword, piercing even to dividing asunder of soul and spirit, and of the joints and marrow, and is a discerner of thoughts and intents of the heart (Hebrews 4:12 KJV).

The carrier is in expectation as a pregnant women waiting for life to come forth. Abraham and Sarah remained childless into their old age. Sarah made an arrangement through Hagar the handmaid despite the Lord's promise to Abraham that He would have children with Sarah (Genesis 17:15-16). In spite of what Sarah did God opened Sarah's womb to carry the **"seed"** which was the promise, Isaac (Genesis 21:3). Originally Sarai, the Lord renamed her Sarah, meaning princess, after she married Abraham. God said, "unto Abraham Sarai thy wife she will not be called Sarai but Sarah shall her name be. I will bless her, and she shall be a mother of nations, kings of people shall be hers". As we see with Abraham even at his age he was to (produce) impregnate Sarah, she conceived at the set time and delivered at the appointed time. Abraham waited with expectation for Sarah to bring forth the child (gift) at the appointed time. Even before this could happen Sarah had to protect what she was carrying for the kingdom. The child was being developed and cared for, nine months for God's perfect will to come forth. God promised Abraham that he would have a son, and Sarah a kingdom carrier brought forth that promise named Isaac.

Isaac **seed** would be innumerable, his seed would possess this land and in his seed will all the nations of the earth be blessed (Genesis 26:3-5). Isaac would then continue to bring forth a kingdom generation that would lead to the genealogy of Jesus Christ. Even Abraham and Sarah realized that God's will was the perfect plan for their life. God's word is about obedience, it's not about reasoning. Obey God's Word! The promises are all in the Word of God. It is very important that we stay tuned to hear God's voice and stay on the same frequency. Kingdom carriers must have spiritual antennas to pick up frequency in the spirit realm so you'll know how to pray and what to pray for through the Holy Spirit. You can now receive transmissions from God. Can you see yourself as a "kingdom carrier"? God is trusting you with kingdom information that has been downloaded into your spirit from the spiritual realm.

Kingdom carriers are very much aware of how they should **"protect the seed"** that they are carrying. Their desire is to wear and model Jesus Christ. There is no casual relationship with Jesus; they are committed to feed the seed with God's word. Jesus is not recycled, nor is He reversed to fit the appetite of the kingdom carrier. The seed is given the authentic Word which increases the nourishment of what is coming forth at the appointed time for delivery.

Rachel the wife of Jacob was definitely a "kingdom carrier". She was carrying a promise child also, Joseph the dreamer who would fulfill God's plan to save a nation. Rachel had been barren the first 26 years of marriage. God, had compassion on her. As the bible records, "God remembered Rachel", and she conceived, **"seed"** Joseph. In Hebrew Joseph name is Yoseph, which means "adding" or "he who adds" (Genesis 30:22-24). Joseph name, also prophetic attest to divine intervention even from the beginning of his life. The dreams of Joseph in Genesis Chapter 37 came true, despite the plotting of his brothers, the lies told by Potiphars wife, and being arrested and put in prison. In spite of all that happened in Genesis Chapters 39 and 40 Joseph was blessed. Rachel was carrying the **"seed"** that God blessed. Everything Joseph set his hands to from his work as a slave in Potiphars house, to his duty in the court prison, and his works as Pharaoh's chief government minister in Egypt God blesses.

The dream of Pharaoh's cup bearer and baker in Genesis Chapter 40 also came true, along with the dream of Pharaoh which foretold the future of Egypt just as Joseph interpreted them. Rachael brought forth the "seed" Joseph that God would use to bring Israel to Egypt and preserve His chosen people during the great famine. God put Israel in a position to grow and prosper, just as Joseph name meant. Joseph story is encouraging for so many reasons even on a personal level. God used hardships to accomplish His plan for the destiny of Joseph.

Hannah another "kingdom carrier" is the wife of Elkanah. The name Hannah speaks of her beauty, it means grace and indeed she is the emblem of grace of womanhood. Hannah became a mother by faith. She appears in I Samuel as a childless woman. Then she becomes a mother, the mother of one of the great men who walked the earth, Samuel. God needed a great women to shape that great man. Samuel was not only the **"seed"**, but a product of the work of God and the product of a "godly mother". Hannah gave to her nation and the world the greatest legacy a woman can ever give, a "godly child". There are several things that stand out about her, (1) a woman of prayer, (2) right relationship with God, (3) right relationship with her husband, (4) right relationship in her home, and (5) dedicated her child back to the Lord.

Elkanah and Hannah (I Samuel 1:1-2, 20) took Samuel at a very young age to Shiloh to consecrate him to the Lord, serving under Eli the priest (I Samuel 1:23, 24; 2:11). Samuel was eventually chosen by God to succeed Eli because Eli's son had become corrupt beyond hope (I Samuel 2:12-26; 3:19-21). After becoming their leader, Samuel turned the Israelites away from their gross idolatry, and led them to an overwhelming victory over the Philistines, who had been severely troubling Israel for over 40 years (I Samuel 7:2-17). Samuel established regular worship of the Lord at Shiloh, where he built an altar, and he established a school of the "prophets" at Ramah, later also at Gibeah, Bethel, Gilgal, and Jericho (I Samuel 3:20-21; II Kings 2:3-5; 4:38). Samuel was another great leader whom God used to bless so many for the kingdom.

Elizabeth the wife of Zechariah and "kingdom carrier", carried the **"seed"** which would be named John the Baptist. Zechariah means God has remembered. Elizabeth is Eli-sheba it means either God's promise, or my God is bountiful/generous. John means "God has been gracious". Elizabeth cousin of Mary of Nazareth was past menopause and her husband Zechariah was elderly. Elizabeth was barren and yet when she conceived she was carrying no ordinary child. His name would be John. John would be great in the sight of God, and he would be filled with the Spirit from conception (Jeremiah 1:5 KJV). John would prepare for the Messiah and thus be a catalyst between Israel and God.

John known as "John the Baptist" was a key figure in the preparation of the Messiah's work. John was the "messenger" who prepares the way. John 1:6 states: Truly, "There came a man, sent from God, whose name was John. A great man from the **"seed"** of Zechariah and Elizabeth, also known as a prophet crying in the wilderness. John's mission can be summed up by one word, "preparer". John came from God in order to **bear witness of the light", Christ** (John 1:7-8).

Seven centuries before the birth of Jesus the prophet Isaiah spoke of "the voice of one that crieth" indeed of him who would "prepare in the wilderness the way of Jehovah" and make level in the desert a highway for our God" (Isaiah 40:3). It is certainly that John's message was from God, and thus infallibly true. The power of John's preaching provided excellent witness to the nature of Christ. John the prophet knew Jesus as the **"Lamb of God" which taketh away the sin of the world** (John 1:29). John emphatically stated that he was not the promised Messiah, nor was he a literally reincarnated Elijah; rather he was the fulfillment of Isaiah's prophecy, the voice of preparation for the arrival of God in the flesh (John 1:19-23). John declared that he was unworthy to either carry Jesus sandals or to unloose the thongs there of (John 1:27), was a stunning testimony indeed with obvious implications. In consideration of the preaching John the immerser baptized Jesus the Messiah, one is Savior of the world. Yes! Jesus the "King of Kings", and "Lord of Lords" who is freely given to all that would believe in Him (Romans 10:9; 13 KJV). His message was concerning Jesus emphasizing upon the coming **"kingdom"** and the warning of ultimate judgment.

Moreover, though John was chronologically older than Jesus, he declared that Christ "was before" him (John 1:15, 30). This past tense form stresses the eternality of the pre-incarnate Word (John 1:1) hence, the Lord's divine essence. John he preached about the coming **"kingdom"** and the need to **"repent"**. John came with his piercing message: **"Repent, for the kingdom of heaven is at hand"** (Matthew 3:2; cf. Mark 1:4). John also proclaimed coming judgment. John's message had a biting edge and he spoke of divine retribution, **"the wrath to come"** (Matthew 3:7). John's mission was to "make ready for the Lord a people prepared" (Luke 1:17). John truly was a great prophet and his life made an impact upon this earth, he was truly a great ingredient in the heavenly plan from God. Let us remember this: Jesus says, *Verily I say unto you, Among them that are born of women there hath not risen a greater than John the Baptist, notwithstanding he that is least in the* **"kingdom of heaven"** *is greater than he* (Matthew 11:11).

In today's society everywhere we look there are warnings from all sectors of life. There are terrorist warnings, economic warnings, health warnings, weather warnings, and even some speak of the end of the world warnings. Some of these warnings are valid, while others are used to simply bring fear on certain people. Our own governmental systems as well as international systems are issuing warnings because of threats by other countries, health agencies also warn of contagious virus/diseases that could spread unless precautions are taken. Economic warnings stem from the markets downfall; from Wall Street, to the banks, automobile industry and housing markets.

There are always the warnings about the weather through meteorologists in monitoring the threats of hurricanes, tornadoes, storms, earthquakes, fires, and other weather related dangers. If you take heed to all these warnings in our world why not take heed to the warnings of God? John himself said, "**Repent! Repent! for the kingdom of God is at hand**". Are you taking heed to the warnings you hear spiritually? Is the warnings you hear from the world system always reliable? Have you ever asked yourself is there a motive behind the ones who are sending the warnings?

Is the warnings really out of concerns for others? Are they preying on peoples fear to sell them something or is this just about getting attention in the headline media? The bible teaches and records many warnings throughout its pages. Those who heeded true warnings from God were spared the predicted consequences. Let's look at what the word "warn" means: to tell (a person) of a danger, coming evil, misfortune, etc: put on guard, caution. Through the history of the world, God has made known to his people impending time of trouble, and given them time to prepare (or escape).

Here are some of the examples listed below:

He warned Noah and his family of the coming flood and directed them how to prepare to survive it. Hebrews 11:7

He warned Lot and his family of the coming destruction of Sodom and Gomorrah. Genesis 19:1;15

He warned the Pharaoh of Egypt, through Joseph, of the coming famine and used Joseph to prepare stores of grain during the 7 years of plenty, which saved Egypt and Joseph's family when a 7 year famine followed the times of plenty. Genesis 41:28-31

He warned the Israelites living under Egyptian slavery that the "angel of death" would kill all the first-born of every family and that they must protect themselves and their families by putting <u>blood of a lamb</u> over the door posts, so the angel would "pass over' them. Exodus 12:23

He warned the wicked people of Nineveh, the capital city of Assyria of God's coming destruction through Jonah. When they <u>repented</u>, the judgment was availed and did not come for a number of years. Jonah 3:1:4;5;10

Jesus said this in regarding the people of Noah's day in Matthew 24:38-39, *"For as in the days that were before the flood they were eating and drinking, marrying and giving in marriage, until the day that Noah entered into the ark. And knew not until the flood came, and took them all away: so shall also the coming of the Son of man be".* Just as John the Baptist (forerunner for Jesus) the **"seed"** from Elizabeth warns the people to **"Repent"** because the time of Christ's coming is unknown, yet all those who choose to repent and believe in Jesus Christ must be ready. The one common denominator is still today just as down through the ages that almost all of those times of trouble the great majority of people could not see the judgments coming. They refused to believe it or that anything could happen to them. They were enjoying the good life (eating, drinking, living immorally, partying) right up until the disaster overtook them. Even today in this 21ˢᵗ Century many are doing exactly the same things if not more. **Now Is the Time! Ask Jesus to Save You Now!** (Romans 10:9;13.)

Are you saved? Are you spiritually prepared for the next warning from God? The greatest preparation that we all need to make is spiritual preparation. Be spiritually prepared: (1) pray (Luke 19:46), (2) study God's word (Romans 10:8; I Timothy 4:6; II Timothy 2:15), (3) have relationships with other believers/share God's word (Hebrews 10:25), (4) share the gospel of Jesus Christ with those who are lost/unsaved (Mark 16:15), (5) have kingdom priorities (Matthew 6:33, Matthew 24:42-51), and watch/pray (Luke 21:30). The true "prophets and prophetesses" of God are still warning of troublous and perilous times coming to this earth which will include more persecution of the saints. As Christian believers we should not fear or doubt God is with us and will protect us (II Timothy 1:7). If you are not **"saved"** then you have a problem, you should be worried. This statement is for those who say they are saved, but not sure, and those who have not yet accepted Jesus Christ as their Savior and Lord.

You have read about several great women who were **"kingdom carriers"** along with their husbands which brought forth the **"seed"** that would also do great things for the **"kingdom of God.** Now lets take a close look at another great woman, Mary the ultimate **"kingdom carrier"** who would carry the "seed" conceived by the power of the Holy Spirit and bring forth the only promise child (Jesus) the Son of God to **save** the world. Mary the wife of Joseph the carpenter, a virgin whom the angel told her that God has found "favor" with. Mary would conceive in her womb and bear a son, and she will name him Jesus. Jesus the Son of God would then come in the "flesh" to show us the way to the Father.

Jesus the teacher, prophet, preacher, healer, and Savior of the world throughout the bible lives and demonstrates to **all** Christian believers how to seek the "kingdom" first while living here on earth (Matthew 6:33 KJV). Jesus teaches principles through parables and effectively gives us "godly wisdom", how believers should occupy until He comes. Jesus spoke the Word and He is the living Word (Genesis 1:1-4; John 1:1-4). Jesus went about all Galilee, teaching in their synagogues, preaching the gospel of the "kingdom", and healing all manner of sickness and disease among the people (Matthew 4:23).

We can observe earlier in Matthew 4:17 the scriptures states: "from that time Jesus begin to **preach,** and to say, *Repent: for the **kingdom of heaven is at hand**.* The word **repent** is found 45 times in the King James Bible. It is evident as Christian believers as we read in our bibles the four gospels Matthew, Mark, Luke, and John teaches us that these writers inspired by the revelation of the Holy Spirit gives us the **"truth"** and **"light"** to **salvation.** Jesus the **"seed"** of Mary by the power of the Holy Spirit gave mankind the only way back to the Father through His life, death, and resurrection. All that Jesus did and spoke was related to the kingdom. Jesus knew it was necessary to demonstrate and live the kingdom here on earth so those who would believe in Him can see. This "kingdom" would lead all to salvation and there is only one way through Jesus. In John 14:6 Jesus saith unto him, *"I am the way, the truth, and the life. No man cometh unto the Father but by me".*

Jesus himself warns the people so they can **"repent"** from their sins and ask for forgiveness. The Savior who stepped out of divinity to come into humanity ("flesh") walked the earth teaching His disciple's kingdom principles and parables how to seek the kingdom and not the things of this world. Jesus our Lord gave advanced **warnings** of the coming persecution to His followers so that they might flee when necessary, prepare for the trials spiritually, or physically, or go underground. Listen to what the Lord is telling you. Wisdom dictates that having some emergency supplies is just the right thing to do. The bible says in II Peter 3:9, "The lord is not slack concerning his promise, as some men count slackness; but is longsuffering to us-ward, not willing that **any should perish,** but that **all should come to repentance.** Jesus warns all people to repent; that is change their mind. Repentance is a change of mind-set which involves the heart. The **blood** of Jesus Christ is the only way men can be redeemed, not by the blood of goats and calves, **but by his own blood,** he entered in once into the holy place, having obtained eternal redemption for us (Hebrews 9:12). Yes! the **"seed"** of Mary conceived by the power of the Holy Spirit gave us Jesus the Savior of the world which no man can come to the Father, but by the Son.

Acts 20:21 speaks of "repentance toward God" and faith toward our Lord Jesus Christ, in which to be **saved** one must turn in faith to Christ alone, believing on him for the forgiveness of sins (Romans 10:9; I John 1:9-10).You see, lost sinners need to repent towards God. You can have all the faith you want as believers and it means nothing because you are in denial about your sins if you don't "repent". The entire message of salvation deals with our sins. Thus, repentance is when you come to the realization that you have sinned against God, and Jesus Christ is the one and only way to be connected back to our Father. Notice in the scripture Mark 1:15 what Jesus said…*"The time is fulfilled,* and the **kingdom of God is** *at hand,* **repent** ye, and **believe** the gospel".

Notice that Jesus didn't say "repent ye, and forsake your sins, **NO** rather He said, **repent** ye, and **believe** the gospel". Either you believe that you must do something to get into heaven or you are simply resting upon Jesus and His precious blood. Are you resting upon Jesus? Repentance is not an option. God commanded us to repent… "And the **times** of this ignorance God winked at: but, now **commandeth all men** every where **to repent"** (Acts 17:30). It is no option whether or not we want to "repent" it is a divine command from Almighty God. II Thessalonians 1:8-9 warns…"In flaming fire taking vengeance on them that know not God and that **obey** not the **gospel** of our Lord Jesus Christ. Who shall be punished with **everlasting destruction** from the presence of the Lord, and from the **glory** of His power.

The road to hell is paved with good intentions, all types of stuff, worldly (fleshly) desires and flashing signs. The road to life is plain and simple yet sometimes can be challenging. The road to **hell exalts religion;** but the road to **heaven exalts Jesus**. There are many types of religions in the world but only **Jesus Christ died for our sins** and was **resurrected** and offers us a loving relationship which leads us back to the **Father.**

This is your life! God has commanded all men to "repent"! Take heed the warning. **Jesus Saves!** Hopefully, you'll die in the Lord. II Corinthians 6:2 says: "For he saith, I have heard thee in a time accepted, and in the day of salvation have I succored thee; behold, now is the accepted time; behold now is the day of salvation. **Now Is the Time!**

As Christians and followers (disciples) of Christ we will always have a relationship with Him as we continue to draw closer and closer towards Him. We are people of His "kingdom" and are connected to the covenant blessings which were given from the beginning with Abraham.

Listed below are scriptures that relate to people of the kingdom (us), in being His children which allows us to be considered heirs of His kingdom, and how He blesses us.

People of the Kingdom

A. <u>His children</u>
Romans 8:16
Galatians 3:26
Galatians 4:6
Philippians 2:15
I John 3:2
II Corinthians 5:17-18

B.<u>Heirs of God</u>
Romans 8:17
Galatians 3:29
Titus 3:7
I Peter 1:4

C.<u>Blessed</u>
Ephesians 1:3
Deuteronomy 28:1-6
Proverbs 10:7
Isaiah 32:20
Acts 20:35
Revelation 14:13

Kingdom Carriers are aware of the promises God has for them, yet they continue to focus on their assignment ahead so they can fulfill their God given purpose and destiny. They have no doubt they are of the kingdom and are rightful heirs to receive the blessings God will bestow upon them. They are aware that God gives us all we need through His presence, power, and promises (II Peter 1:4-6). Just as God gives us all we need we must also bring something to the table. We also have a role to play in bringing what is necessary to become all that God has created us to be. Kingdom carriers have the passionate desire to be all God wants them to be. As children of God we want His values and standards so we are able to hold up or stand under what ever pressure that comes against us. We have the faith and knowledge to believe God's word through any and everything we face. We should have self-control, patience and endurance under pressure which are valuable spiritual dynamics in our steadfastness.

Ephesians 3:20-21 clearly states: Now unto him that is able to do exceeding abundantly above all that we ask or think, according to the power that worketh in us. Unto him be glory in the church by Christ Jesus throughout all ages, world without end. Amen.

God has the appointed time to fulfill the vision, dreams, and desires in your heart. Just because it has taken a long time or you're tired of waiting doesn't mean it's not going to happen. There is something inside of you that God wants to bring forth (deliver). Your perspective of God must always be greater than your reality (perspective is what you perceive things to be). Jeremiah 33:3 lets us see that God wants to show you His vision for your life. He will unfold it for you, the step of obedience it requires, so get steady on your feet and watch God use you to carry what He has already placed in you from the foundation of the world. Just as God was with Gideon in Judges

Chapter 6:11-16 and so many others in the bible we read about who were called to do something for the kingdom, He will take care of you also because He desires that you have a hope and a future that leads to an expected end (Jeremiah 29:11 KJV).

God's desire is to bring forth what He has put in you before the foundations of the world. You are a "kingdom carrier" and just as God used so many of the great men and women mentioned throughout the bible He will do the same with you. Go forward you are a child of God and He knows your heart.

Chapter 4 Questions and Exercises

1. What are you carrying for the "kingdom of God"?

2. Knowing who you are and what God has called you to is very important. Can you identify the 7 "I AM" in the gospel of John which relates to Jesus? Write them on the lines below.

   _____

   _____

3. Name five "kingdom carriers" from the Old Testament and New Testament.

   _____

   _____

   _____

4. Jeremiah Chapter 1 verse 5 quotes these words of scripture text. Write the scripture from memory.

5. Why is it important to protect what you are carrying inside for the "kingdom of God'?

6. Name the five women who were "kingdom carriers"? What is the name of their "seed" (child) who did great things for the kingdom of God?

7. Where in scripture does John the Baptist and Jesus Christ our Savior and Lord say "repent" for the kingdom of heaven is at hand"?

8. In what Chapter and verses of scripture does God change Abram name to Abraham and Sarai name to Sarah?

9. Fill in the missing word: Know who you _____; Know who's in _____; Know your _____; Know your _____; and Know your _____.

10. Look at the following scriptures: Acts 17:30; Matthew 3:7; II Thessalonians 1:8-9 and II Corinthians 6:2. Study and write down from memory these scriptures below.

_____

_____

_____

_____

"**Ask Jesus to save you now and have eternal life**". **Dear Lord Jesus I repent of my sins; Come into my heart and save me. I believe Romans 10:9 which says: That if thou shalt confess with thy mouth the <u>Lord Jesus</u>, and shalt believe in thine heart that God hath raised him from the dead, thou <u>shalt be saved.</u> "For whosoever shall call upon the name of the <u>Lord shall be saved</u> (Romans 10:13).**

CHAPTER 5

Kingdom Assignment

*Go ye therefore and teach all nations, baptizing them in the name of Father, and
of the Son, and of the Holy Ghost. Teaching them to observe all things whatsoever I
have commanded you: and lo, I am with you always, even unto the end of the world.
Amen.*
Matthew 28:19-20

Most of us if not all have asked these questions: Who am I? Why am I here? Where do I go
from here? And how do I get there? Only because of your relationship with God these questions
have been answered through the leading and guiding by the Holy Spirit. Some still may not quite
know the answer to these questions because they have not sought God nor have they desired to
know what their kingdom assignment is. The essence of everything we do in our assignments must
be through prayer. First, God who you pray to, second, people who you pray for, and third people
you pray with. We must have good communication with God for service in His kingdom. Always
allow the Holy Spirit to say what should be said when you are on your kingdom assignment. Your
kingdom assignment may involve many facets such as leadership, living as light, kingdom wealth,
and going wherever God has commanded you to go.

The scripture tells us in Genesis 1:26, And God said, "Let us make man in our image after
our likeness: and let them have dominion over the fish of the sea, and over the fowl of the air, and
over the cattle, and over all the earth, and over every creeping thing that creepeth upon the earth".
Jeremiah 1:5 states: Before I formed thee in the belly I knew thee: and before thou camest forth
out of the womb I sanctified thee, and I ordained thee a prophet unto the nations (KJV). Whether
you are apart of the five-fold ascension gifts or not God has created all of us for His purpose and
His glory. We were created to know the love of God and show the love of God in all we do in the
earth realm. Through our daily life while God's word is transforming us to the image of Christ,

He is preparing us for our kingdom assignments. You're probably thinking what is my kingdom assignment and how do I know if it's an assignment from God? Your kingdom assignment is whenever and where ever God sends you through the leading of the Holy Spirit.

The assignment can be in your home, on your job, market place, at school, eating at a restaurant, riding on public transportation, praying for family members/friends, praying for church leaders/body, praying for the lost, the afflicted, addicted, oppressed, suppressed, and depressed in the earth realm. It may be also praying for nations, praying for the educational systems, political/governmental systems, and economic systems of this world. Everyone has a different assignment and it can be any and everywhere you come in contact with people, yes even at church! Why do you think you have the personality you have? It's no accident let me assure you. You are not a mistake! God has created you for the assignment. God has given us our personalities to be used as a resource for His purpose.

Have you ever analyzed your personality? Why not simply examine your strengths and weaknesses of your personality traits. Remember this is why whatever God uses us to do He gives us the strength and power to do it because He knows our weaknesses. Paul says in Philippians 4:13, "I can do all things through Christ that strengtheneth me" and also in II Corinthians 12:10, "Therefore I take pleasure in infirmities, in reproaches, in necessities, in persecutions, in distresses, for Christ's sake: for when I am weak, then I am strong. In this text of scripture to the Corinthians Paul mentioned his experiences because they were bragging about their own spiritual visions and gifts, yet Paul in humility wanted to demonstrate to them that he had a spiritual experience far superior to anything they had encountered. It's not the things we do for Christ will last, but only the things we do through Christ will last.

Our lives should always reflect as though we're on an assignment from God. Paul states in Philippians 2:13, "For it is God which worketh in you both to will and to do of *his* good pleasure". There is a kingdom assignment that God wants to use you strategically for and only you can do that particular assignment because of what God has placed inside of you (His word and His power). As Christian believers on any assignment we must always walk in the light and let our light shine before men. Don't hide the light, cover the light up, or put the light out (I John 1:5 KJV). Never forget the bible within the bible!

John 3:16 states: *"For God so loved the world, that he gave his only begotten Son, that whosoever believeth in him should not perish, but have everlasting life. For God sent not his Son into the world to condemn the world; but that the world through him might be **saved**."*

We must always be ready and stay knowledgeable of God's word so we can be available to share the Romans Road while during our assignments. The Romans Road consist of the following scriptures of text: Romans 3:10; Romans 3:23; Romans 5:8; Romans 5:12; Romans 6:23; Romans

10:9; Romans 10:10; and Romans 10:13, which this road leads unbelievers to salvation. The Holy Spirit may lead you to say Jesus loves you to a stranger and you have still filled your kingdom assignment. As I mentioned earlier in this chapter the kingdom assignment is not always the same assignment. It can be difficult or seem difficult but God knows what you can handle. God would never put on you no more than you can bear (I Corinthians 10:13 KJV). Christian believers must never forget or have selected amnesia in knowing that God has given us power through the Holy Spirit, and we are kingdom leaders called to expose, cancel out, eradicate, and annihilate the very powers of darkness in the spiritual realm so victory can manifest in the earthly realm.

As a kingdom carrier you now have set your mind on the kingdom assignment which involves walking by faith and not by sight (II Corinthians 5:7 KJV). In other words we believe it before we see it. Ephesians 3:20-21 states: "Now to Him who is able to do far more abundantly beyond all that we ask or think, according to the power that works within us; to Him be the glory in the church and in Christ Jesus to all generations forever and ever" (NAS).

As I reflect on the days of being in school many assignments were always given by the teachers or professors. Most of the time they were fun to do and other times they were challenging, yet I was responsible to make sure they were completed so I could pass the class. This is the educational system of the world in which we follow to fulfill our academic achievements/ portfolio. Now since the years have gone by as a follower (disciple) of Christ and being a part of the kingdom of God it's been revealed that I have a kingdom assignment. You also have a kingdom assignment that God has either revealed to you or will reveal to you. The more and more I sought the Lord the closer and closer I grew and experienced His love for me. I was then given revelation, knowledge by the power of the Holy Spirit to lead and guide me as I travel the journey ahead. When God sent me on my assignments for the kingdom I was prepared for what He had called me to do whether the assignment was to share the gospel in many ways with family members/friends, by standing on the street corners sharing Jesus, convalescent homes, juvenile prison, market place, job, riding on a airplane, preaching in a church or volunteering through different community events. The assignments must be complete because they are very important for the kingdom cause. It's all about **souls being saved**!

Some assignments may be places you don't even want to go or feel you can't do, but remember it is not about you, it is about Him and His purpose. The Holy Spirit knows where to lead you. As you travel on your journey of kingdom assignments you will encounter those who are willing to spread the gospel, some who will hinder the gospel, and those who adorn the gospel. Here are three examples found in III John which tells us Gauis would spread the gospel, Diotrephes would hinder the gospel, and Demetrius would adorn the gospel. Gauis was one who held on to the truth of Jesus Christ and the Christian faith (III John verses 3, 4). He was very active in the church assisting Christian missionaries on their journey. Gauis doing his assignment faced unjustly behavior and was mistreated by a prominent church leader of his congregation named Diotrephes (III John verses

9, 10). Diotrephes forbid members like Gaius to assist the missionaries who traveled. Unlike the behavior of Diotrephes, the scriptures tell us again of another person Demetrius, who had worked faithfully to spread the gospel of Jesus and is noted as such a good man from God (III John verse 12). These men were willing to stay on their assignments regardless of what they endured for the gospel of Jesus Christ.

The journey will continue as you do what God has called you to do. You may find yourself where God has sent you and your very presence in a room (atmosphere) speak volumes just because of who you are and the power of the Holy Spirit that dwells within. Literally you don't have to say anything and others will be drawn to Jesus through you and converts will be **saved**. Yes, allow the Holy Spirit to guide you for the appropriate time to share the gospel. Remember the scripture tells us in I Corinthians 15:58, "Therefore, my beloved brethren, be ye steadfast, unmovable, always abounding in the work of the Lord, forasmuch as ye know that your labor is not in vain in the Lord." (KJV)

Kingdom Leadership

Kingdom leadership will always require that you walk holy before a Holy God. The bible says in Leviticus 11:44 "For I *am* the Lord your God: ye shall therefore sanctify yourselves, and ye shall be holy: for I *am* holy: neither shall ye defile yourselves with any manner of creeping thing that creepeth upon the earth." (Leviticus 19:2; 20:7; and I Peter 1:15-16 KJV). Leadership can be defined as the position and ability to lead (someone who has followers). A kingdom leader lifestyle should include fasting/praying, studying the Word of God and having the time for resting, and balance between spending time with your family and doing what God has called you to do. As a leader you are to never neglect yourself, your family or the responsibilities that God has given you to take care of. So many leaders think this is okay to do and some are simply just confused because the more they do for the ministry the more they feel they have pleased God through their labor for the kingdom. Not so! God does not want or require us to neglect what is important to Him which is our families and doing our assignments.

Leaders do need to rest and be refreshed. Take time to seek the Lord and remove yourself from anyone or anything that will stop you from being in the presence of God. Even Moses realized that he needed to take a break to go before the presence of God. Jesus our Lord and Savior also went before the Father. This is a time to be spiritually fed while gaining physical rest so you will be able to complete your assignment which will bring glory to God. A time where God is giving you exactly what you need so when you return from spending time with Him his glory will be all over you.

As kingdom leaders we walk in love, holiness, humility, integrity, obedience, truth, forgiveness, compassion, and righteousness through the power of the Holy Spirit. Jesus Christ the one and only kingdom leader, who is the Kingdom shows us how to live out all these characteristics of a Christian leader. We must always walk in the "light" and not in "darkness". Kingdom leadership will always require that you die to the **flesh** and be ready in season for spiritual battles. You must be able to discern along with knowing the "times and seasons" (And the children of Issachar, which were men that had understanding of the times, to know what Israel ought to do, the heads of them were two hundred; and all their brethren were at their commandment) I Chronicles 12:32; ref: Esther 1:13; KJV. Many leaders in the bible had to go on the battlefield so their assignment would be completed for the purpose of fulfilling what the scriptures reveals to us as we learn and live by God's word.

Kingdom leaders should be clothed in righteousness, and modeling Jesus (Romans 13:14). Are you wearing and modeling Jesus in your marriage, with your family, in your home, on your job, and in your school? We should say Jesus tailor me and let me model you for the "kingdom" here on earth. As leaders we should be committed to Jesus, yet some leaders want to be casual with Jesus, recycle Jesus, and reverse Jesus. Wearing Jesus on your shoulder is not the way to go, you shouldn't put Him on whenever you desire (Matthew 23:28). Jesus should always be in our hearts because remember you are a leader for the "kingdom" of God. This is not by chance that God has call/chosen you to lead. Make the decision to always be clothed in Jesus. He is the only designer worth wearing.

Walking In the Light

Light is how Christian leaders and believers must walk to dispel darkness. We walk in the "light" (phos) because Jesus is the light and there is no "darkness" (skotia) in Him. Light is illumination, walking in the understanding, the right attitude, and right knowledge of God. God's light illuminates and make things clear. The Hebrew word for light (phos) is never kindled and therefore never quenched contrary to darkness (skotia) thus is not a figurative term for sin, but refers to the consequences of sin. The scripture clearly states in Ephesians 5:8, "For ye were sometimes darkness, but now are ye light in the Lord; walk as children of light. The way we live and where ever we walk the "illumination" of His light shines brightly on us and around us. I John 1:5-7 clearly states: that God is light, and in him is no darkness at all. If we say that we have fellowship with him, and walk in darkness, we lie, and do not the truth. But if we walk in the light, as he is in the light, we have fellowship one with another, and **the blood of Jesus Christ his Son cleanseth us from all sin.** As we see in these scriptures of text John gives us three major points which explains (1) that God is "light" symbolizing absolute purity and holiness, (2) how believers can walk in God's light and have fellowship with him, and (3) to dispel doubts and to build assurance by presenting a clear picture of Jesus Christ.

Jesus said, *"I Am the Light of the World"* he that followed me shall not walk in darkness but shall have the light of life (John 8:12 KJV). God has commanded us to "go ye therefore" in doing our assignment yet we must understand in kingdom leadership our focus here in the text is spiritual light. This light is not natural light or artificial light. Understand that man must examine who God is in relation to who man is. Man is the creation of God and must acknowledge His superiority over him (Genesis 1:27 says; so God created man in his own image). When you're walking in the light, you have a kingdom agenda on a kingdom assignment. Jesus was about the kingdom, doing his Father's business. He had already destroyed Satan, and Jesus has all power in heaven and earth. Christian leaders and believers have that same power (Luke 10:19-20). We are Christ in the earth realm.

Some Christians are often in the same predicament as non-Christians. We live in a dimly lighted world, where **sin** is the rule and there are no other expectations, and yet we are children of the light. Believers must always be on our guard that we do not become so accustomed to the darkness of this world that we think it is normal and conform to its guidelines. It is not normal. The dim moral and spiritual insight of the world is not the standard that the Christian is to walk by (Matthew 5:13-16). We should come up to God's standards rather expect God to come down to ours, which He never will. Un-believers of this world are proud, self-sufficient, and do not understand their own unrighteousness before a Holy God. Before we can discuss how a believer can influence the world, we have to examine what type of people are believers. Jesus described these people in Matthew 5:3-12, and we have come to know these verses as the Beatitudes. As believers and follower of Christ we must always walk in the "light" while doing our assignments for the kingdom of God.

As a Christian believer walking in the light you can't be rooted and grounded in your material possessions (things), people you see on t.v., your custom made tailor suits, houses, cars, or money. Believers must maintain a sense of balance in what God has called us to do since the foundation of the earth. God is raising up His true remnant with the power of the Holy Spirit residing in them that will lead the way to help others who are saved come back to the Word, come back to Jesus, come back to holiness, and come back to fasting and praying. Also God will use His remnant to bring the lost (sinner) unto Him through His Son, the Savior Jesus Christ. They will be **saved.** The remnant will also share the gospel (good news) by any means necessary through the power that worketh in them to those who are in need of a Savior. As God continues to use you doing your assignments, you must see God clearly, see yourself clearly, and others clearly which is one way that can help you can grow in the Spirit. Know that God is using you for His kingdom here on earth. Everything you need is already inside of you. In order to do what God says, you need to have a "vertical" relationship first which involves God speaking and you listening. Revelation 4:1 says: "After this I looked, and behold, a door was opened in heaven and the first voice which I heard was as it were of a trumpet talking with me; which said, Come up hither, and I will show thee things which must be hereafter".

Even John saw Him as one in the Spirit and that our wholeness is to be one. Galatians Chapter 5 teaches us the privileges of Christian liberty and we're not to walk as the world in darkness but walk as children of light. We walk and live in the fruit of the Spirit. There is a place within us only God fills and only God can complete us (not a person). It's about being authentic, no more posing, and posturing, and no more playing before other people. It's about being authentic! **Jesus is authentic!**

Christian believers must also understand that being in the world, but not of it is necessary if we are to be a light to those who are in spiritual darkness. We are to live in such a way that those outside the faith see our good deeds and our manna and know that there is something "different" about us. Christians who make every effort to live and act like those who do not know Christ do Him a great disservice. Even some un-believers (sinners), know the scripture "by their fruits you shall know them" and as Christians, we should exhibit the fruits of the Spirit within us (Galatians 5:22-25). We are shining lights in a dark world; we are to shine where ever God leads us in doing our assignments for His "kingdom"

We must examine ourselves and have no motives behind what God has called or chosen us to do for His kingdom. Every human being knows that there is a God even if they don't admit it. He has created it in us to know He exist (Romans 8:29-30). Believers should be lighting the dark places not conforming to the world. Let your light shine! Don't turn your light off to compromise darkness! Remember you should have a "kingdom" mind-set. It's all about the "kingdom" now!

John 17:14-15; Cross References: I John 5:19; John 12:31; John 16:11

<u>Deception of darkness</u>

Whatever assignments God has called us to do there will always be the deceiver (Satan) waiting to entice us with fleshly desires which leads to consequences of **sin.** Romans 5:8 declares: "But God demonstrated His own love toward us in that while we were still sinners, Christ died for us". **<u>Jesus Christ died for us</u>**! Jesus death paid for the price of our **sins**. Jesus resurrection proves that God accepted Jesus death for our sins. Don't allow darkness to put out the light! Many leaders and believers have fallen doing their assignment for God. The flesh has been allowed to be fed with an overdose of worldly desires. Relationships have been destroyed because of sexual immorality, homosexual lovers/liaisons, fraud, seduction of young converts and members all in the body of Christ, because many have lost their focus on what their assignment really is. Be not deceived! I also must point out that God is a loving and forgiving God when a (believer) individual truly ask and seek repentance from Him. Romans 3:23 says: "For all have sinned and come short of the glory of God". We have all sinned. Romans 3:10-18 gives a detailed picture of what sin looks like in our lives. We can't afford to sin anymore because we have now chosen to walk in the **"light"**. We live holy and the deception of darkness has no hold on us.

God has called you to do great things for His kingdom, yet the enemy will try to stop you at all cost. Satan doesn't care about our title, position, wealth, or prestige his desire is to totally destroy what God has put inside of us before the foundation of the world. Deception of darkness comes in all forms, types, colors, and shapes. Our flesh must be crucified (kill) on a daily basis so we don't succumb to the darkness of this world (Romans 8:12-14; Galatians 5:24).

Anything we do in our assignments for the kingdom will always require God's help and the power of the Holy Spirit. Stay focused! Don't allow the veil of deception to cover your heart. God has not prepared us to be defeated. God has a plan for you and me. Fear is one of the enemy's favorite tools of deception to keep us from going forward in the kingdom assignment God has told us to do. As soon as we make a decision to step out in faith and do what God is telling us to do, immediately the enemy will bring the deception of fear.

The enemy will put thoughts in your mind like; "What if I fail? What will others think? Or maybe I don't have what it takes to do this job. He will do his best to use fear and doubt to convince you not to go forward which will stunt spiritual growth and progress. The deception of darkness through fear wages a battle in your mind so much that it starts to consume your thoughts. The bible tells us that fear is a spirit. Proverbs 29:25 says: "Fear of man will prove to be a snare, but whosoever trusts in the Lord is kept safe" (NIV). The spirit of fear affects your emotions, but when you choose to put your trust in the Lord no matter how you are feeling, you are combating fear. The world systems will also bring all kinds of deception against Jesus our Lord and Savior and use it against every believer. Regardless, of how society has distorted and portrayed the image of Christ, we have been created by God to be a light in the earth and followers (disciples) of Christ. The keys and answers to our victory in fulfilling every assignment have already been given to us in the bible. Walk in the "light" for your kingdom assignment will always destroy the powers of darkness.

As mentioned, earlier in this chapter concerning the Romans Road to Salvation listed below are some scriptures that will help you always remember the blessings God has given us through the dead and resurrection of His, Son Jesus Christ Our Lord and Savior. **Jesus gave His all that we would live (eternally).**

Romans Road to Salvation

I. Romans 3:23: For **all have sinned**, and come short of the glory of God. We have all sinned. Romans 3:10-18 gives a detailed picture of what sin looks like in our lives.
II. Romans 6:23: For the wages of sin is death; but the gift of God is eternal life through Jesus Christ our Lord: this verse teaches us that there is consequences to **sin**. This is not just physical death but eternal death. (spiritual)
III. Romans 5:8: declares "But God demonstrated His own love toward us, in that while we were still sinners, Christ died for us! Jesus death paid for the price of our sins. Jesus resurrection proves that God accepted Jesus death as the payment for **all our sins**.
IV. Romans 10:9: that if you confess with your mouth Jesus as Lord, and believe in your heart that God raised Him form the dead, you will be **saved**.

V. Romans 10:13 says it again, For whosoever shall call upon the name of the Lord shall be **saved**.

VI. Romans 5:1: Therefore, being justified by faith, we have peace with God through our Lord Jesus Christ.

VII. Romans 8:1 teaches us, There is therefore now no condemnation to them which are in Christ Jesus, who walk not after the flesh, but after the spirit.

God has given us His promises in Romans 8:38-39. "For I am persuaded, that neither death, nor life, nor angels, nor principalities, nor powers, nor things present, nor things to come. Nor height, nor depth, nor any other creature, shall be able to separate us from the love of God, which is in Christ Jesus our Lord.

Have you ever shared the Romans Road with anyone? Many believers may have not shared the Romans Road and some may have not even been aware or taught these scriptures of text. However, regardless of how the Holy Spirit leads you to share the gospel of Jesus Christ while doing your assignments know that he who wins souls is wise (Proverbs 11:30-31).

Kingdom leadership will always require that you be ready for battle. If there's one thing that can lead you down the road away from your journey and following the awesome plan God has for your life, its emotions. God has given us all emotions, yet oftentimes we allow our problems or circumstances to dictate our emotions and thoughts instead of the Word of God. Just take a look at II Chronicles Chapter 20 when Jehoshaphat had to go into battle the emotion of fear came in because of knowing there was a great multitude that was coming up against them. Jehoshaphat set himself to seek the Lord, and proclaimed a fast throughout all Judah. Leaders must know they can always seek God for direction through the leading of the Holy Spirit. Praying and fasting can be crucial in fighting every spiritual battle. Knowing how to discern and try the spirits (I John 4:1-6) is also something a kingdom leader must know how to do. Never forget that many throughout the 66 books of the bible went through some type of spiritual battle because they were called as leaders to do their assignment for the kingdom of God.

The bible says when we allow doubt and fear in we become unstable. We are tossed back and forth! "But when he asks, he must believe and not doubt, because he who doubts is like a wave of the sea, blown and tossed by the wind" (Mark 11:23). We get upset by what we see or hear sometimes and this opens the door for doubt and fear. Don't allow yourself to be tossed around by your emotions any longer. Choose to have a kingdom mind-set and follow the plans of God for your life.

Kingdom leadership requires leader's to minister life to Christian believers, not by being judgmental but by speaking the gospel truth. Leaders must not neglect the flock (sheep) that God has placed them over nor hurt the flock in anyway. You are not allowed or entitled to go around sleeping with members in the church or outside the church, married or single. Seducing new young converts, having multiple liaison lovers, are embezzling funds from the house of God it is not a part of you kingdom leadership duties. Boastfulness and pride is not needed or wanted, but kingdom leadership does demand you must have a spirit of humility, compassion, and servanthood for others. Leadership involves integrity, truth, walking up-right before God, and repentance when you need to go to God and others for forgiveness.

David said in Psalm 51:9-13 that he wanted a clean heart, he was praying to God for spiritual cleansing. God loves us so much that He will forgive! Just ask with a sincere heart! This is one of the greatest passages in the bible concerning confession and forgiveness. It was written after David had committed adultery with Bath-sheba and subsequently had her husband Uriah killed in battle (see II Samuel 11:2-17).

Some who are in leadership positions are still refusing to **repent** or acknowledge they have even sinned before God. We can't afford to walk in light and darkness at the same time. You can't have one foot in the kingdom and one foot in the world. This totally contradicts the message of the gospel of Jesus Christ. The book of Amos 3:3 clearly states: Can two walk together, except they be agreed? **Repent! Repent!** For the kingdom of God is at hand. Jesus Loves You! Yes, Jesus forgives!

Jesus our Lord and Savior was on His assignment for the kingdom, yet He is the kingdom of God. In Luke 4:43 Jesus quotes: "And he said unto them, *I must preach the kingdom of God to other cities also; for therefore am I sent.* He preached in the synagogues of Galilee (Luke 4: 44). Jesus never forgot what he was to do in the earth realm. The priority was all about the kingdom of God which is what His assignment was about. When we look from the perspective of Luke Chapter 2:48 he describes Mary and Joseph's reaction to finding Jesus among the teachers in the temple as being amazed. The Greek verb is ekplesso, "to cause to be filled with amazement to the point of being overwhelmed", "be amazed, dumbfounded."

Jesus at twelve years old was so engaged in doing what he had been chosen to do. Joseph and Mary were concerned with worry because they found him not with them on the journey. Jesus tarried behind in Jerusalem. Joseph and Mary turned backed again to Jerusalem seeking him. His parent's finally spots him. It came to past, that after three days they found him in the temple, sitting inn the midst of the teachers both hearing them, and asking them questions. Although they were amazed, his mother said to him Son, why have you treated us like this? Your father and I have been anxiously searching for you. After Mary sees that Jesus is safe, her motherly instinct takes over.

In Luke 2:49 Jesus quotes: "And he said unto them, *How it that ye sought me? wist ye not that I must be about my Father's business.*" The emphasis is on the word "must". I must be about my Father's business, in the things of my Father with a determination. This verse illustrates and refers to the necessity of Jesus being involved in the instruction from God, given what He is doing. Jesus was determined to do what pleases his Father. Joseph and Mary didn't understand what Jesus spoke unto them. There is no doubt in which Luke shares through biblical scriptures that Jesus knew what His priority was. The assignments that God has given us must be taken very seriously and we are to fulfill what God has called us to do. Are we about our Father's business?

As men and woman called by God we must know our "assignment". There are many ministers trying to preach the gospel but are not in the right assignment. Many believers are just doing things because they see others in the body of Christ doing something. Whether you're in leadership or not you must know what your assignment is from God. How can you effectively do what God has called you to do without the anointing power of the Holy Spirit? It is of naught! Stay in your own assignment! Stay in position! Resist the desire to be someone else or somewhere else. Be content with your assignment and be convinced that it only takes the power of God to change people. It's not your preaching, teaching, prophesying, healing/deliverance it's the power of God. Paul was used to preach only the power and demonstration of God (Romans 1:14-16 KJV).

There were other examples that John the revelator taught us concerning the importance of Jesus going about doing his assignment for his Father. Jesus again quotes: in John 4:34: *"My meat is to do the will of him that sent me, and to finish his work"*. The disciples saying, Master eat but he said to them *"I have meat to eat that ye know not of"*. (John 4:32). Jesus was speaking to them from a kingdom perspective. The scripture in John 5:36 states another quote of Jesus saying, *"But I have greater witness than that of John: for the works which the Father hath given me to finish, the same works that I do, bear witness of me, that the Father hath sent me"*. Jesus teaches us and shows a clear picture from the gospel writings of Luke and John how He was about doing His kingdom assignment for his Father and what really matters. The eternal message will always last and lead to everlasting life.

Commanded to Go!

Are you fulfilling your "kingdom commission"? **Now is the Time! Go!** The word "go" in Greek means: "hupago" which means "to depart, get hence, go a(-way)". We are the voice of His word, we have His word in us and must vocalize it. Now is the time for our lights to shine! Isaiah 60:1-2 says: Arise, shine: for they light is come, and the glory of the Lord is risen upon thee. For, behold, the darkness shall cover the earth, and gross darkness the people; but the Lord shall arise upon thee, and his glory shall be seen upon thee. We're the "remnant" that's going to live and voice what we believe. We're going to stand for what is right so everyone can see Jesus as they may. As salt and light in the world we have the anointing and power of God as kingdom carriers to **"go into all the world"**. Bringing the "good news" (gospel) to a perverse and twisted generation those that are lost in need of a Savior (Philippians 2:15). Jesus words with the disciples in Luke 24:47 says that *"forgiveness of sins should be preached to all nations";* clearly indicate His concern for the nations (ethne-peoples) from the beginning.

Jesus repeated this "command" to the disciples in Acts 1:8. This verse illuminates the scope of the "command" by noting geographic and cultural barriers through which the gospel must "go" in order to satisfy God's heart for the nations.

Christian believers have a responsibility to follow the "great commission", command Jesus gave to all of us; "go into all the world and make disciples" (Matthew 28:19). I think we need God's perspective of where the "world" is and who is sent to go. The power to do it is ours through the Holy Spirit. The command to do it is absolutely clear from our Savior. Acts 1:8 identifies where you are going whether its Jerusalem (local), Judea (state, country, nation), Samaria (going places where no one would go), end of the earth (going to all the countries) and undesirable places. Are you and I covering our corners of the world? If we don't, no one will. What would happen in our land if every Christian in the working world viewed their jobs as their mission field (assignment from God)? I challenge you to get serious about your corner of the world and see what God has called you to do for His "kingdom" here on earth. This is an **"urgent call to go"**! **Just do it!**

Peter and Paul went to different communities and different places just as so many others in the bible. You have been commanded to go! Don't let anyone or anything convince you that you are not capable of what God told you to do. Learn to accept the assignment God has given you. Remember that the gospel is not about being popular it's about being effective. Don't let people label you! David was a little shepherd boy out in the field tending to his "daddy's" sheep, yet he was the one who became King. Rahab a women of the streets, but later became a woman highly favored. Like, David God will take you from the background to a place of influence and just like Rahab she was used to stop a generational curse. Even Jesus couldn't do miracles in His home town, they said isn't that Jesus the carpenter's son? They labeled Jesus by his past and said don't believe all that you've heard, that's just Jesus. Yes! they even labeled Jesus and He is the Savior and Son of God. People from your past can't accept who you are so they label you in spite of what you've become. You have an assignment from God to do in the earth realm, **go and do it!** (Ephesians 3:20 KJV)

When some believers look at you from a worldly mind-set based on the exterior appearances God looks at you from the interior because it's the "heart" that matters. Just look from the perspective of David's life how God called him from among them and yet chosen him from them. God knew David had a "kingdom assignment" to fulfill in the earth realm.

God is getting ready to show you what to do, when to do it, and how to do it. God is the only one you should be listening to through the direction and leading of the Holy Spirit (Romans 8:14-17). Get up and go whenever and wherever God sends you. Everything you need is within you. God will never send you anywhere unprepared. God has equipped and prepared you to go through His word, His will, His purpose, and His power. What ever God has commanded you to do, just **go and do it.** You have been "anointed" to do what God has called you to do. Isaiah 61 says: The Spirit of the Lord God is upon me; because the Lord hath **anointed** me to preach good tidings unto the meek: he hath sent me to bind up the broken; hearted, to proclaim liberty to the captives, and the opening of the prison to them that are bound: To proclaim the acceptable year of the Lord, and the day of vengeance of our God, to comfort all that mourn. (KJV)

Now let's take a look at some of the individuals God told to **"go"**.

Genesis 7:1 The Lord then said to Noah, "**Go** into the ark, you and your whole family, because I have found you righteous in this generation." The ark was built by Noah so God could rescue Noah and his family, along with pairs of every animal. God will provide, He will guide , the Lord is our healer.

Exodus 3:10-13 God tells Moses, "I am sending you to Pharaoh to lead my people out of Egypt. **Go**! Moses protest, "Who am I to do this job?" God answer, It is not who you are, but who I Am. I will be with you!

Joshua 6:3-4 The Lord told Joshua to **go** to Jericho and to march seven times around the walls. He followed faithfully and obeyed the Lord's command.

Judges 7:8-9 "So Gideon sent the rest of the Israelites to their tents but kept the three hundred, who took over the provisions and trumpets of the others. Now the camp of Midian lay below him in the valley. During that night the Lord said to Gideon, "Get up, **go** down against the camp, because I am going to give it into your hands.

I Samuel 23:2 Therefore David inquired of the Lord, saying: Shall I go and smite these Philistines? And the Lord said unto David, **Go**, and smite the Philistines, and save Keilah.

I Kings 17:8-9 says: "Then the Lord said to Elijah, "**Go** and live in the village of Zarephath, near the city of Sidon. There is a widow there who will feed you. I have given her my instructions." Elijah was on his assignment from God. During the three and one-half years of drought, God always directed him where to **go** and what to do. God commanded a widow to feed him on his journey. (I Kings 17:9). There is an exact place where God wants you to be so He can sustain and bless you.

II Kings 1:15 And the angel of the Lord said unto Elijah, **Go** down with him: be not afraid of him. And he arose, and went down with him unto the king.

Matthew 26:36-39,42 Then cometh Jesus with them unto a place called Gethsemane, and saith unto the disciples, Sit ye here while I **go** and pray yonder. Jesus prayed saying, O my Father, if it be possible, let this cup pass from me; nevertheless not as I will, but as thou wilt. He went again the second time, and prayed saying, O Father, if this cup may not pass away from me, except I drink it, thy will be done.

As Christian believers we have often heard "Where God guides, He provides." We must always remain ready to **"go"** to the place God leads us. (Scripture References: I Kings 17:2-7; 17:8-9; Joshua 1:1-3; Psalm 134:1-3; Acts 10:24-48)

This assignment was given to the body of Christ not the secular charities, not the government. God wants to bring forth the manifestation and demonstration of His glory and power in the earth realm through those He has called/chosen for such a time as this. Its time out for tea parties and fashion shows, you have been strategically chosen and ordained to do your "kingdom assignment" before you were created in your mother's womb. Don't fear! Fear is only false evidence appearing real. Joshua teaches us in Chapter1 verse 6-7 and 9 the call to be strong and of good courage which really is a call to faith. Believing God's promises would lead both to courage and obedience.

Here's something to think about remember there are three kinds of people: (1) people who make things happen, (2) people who watch things happen, and (3) people who don't know what happen. Which one are you? Stop making excuses, complaining I can't **go**, I'm not qualified, I'm to young or old, I can't leave my family, or simply just being rebellious and won't go. You must go! The world is waiting for you. Some places you have to go alone, but just "go". Remember, the Holy Spirit is with you and in you. God can even send a team with you to help if He chooses to, but use discernment to make sure the right people are on the team. Amos 3:3 says: Can two walk together, except they be agreed?

Obedience verses Opposition

We are the "remnant" generation that will be obedient to what God has called and chosen us to do. It will happen quickly! It's time for God's people to take their rightful place so the remnant God has put on this earth from the beginning can advance the kingdom. **Now Is the Time!** Open the door, God wants you to do something, go have faith to do it. In Acts Chapter 9 verses 10-18 God showed Ananias what to do and where to go and Saul was waiting. God showed Ananias and Saul one to another in a vision. They both were obedient to do what God had showed them in the vision. Ananias then laid his hands on Saul. Saul eyes were opened and the scales were removed. Ananias was on his kingdom assignment and Saul was the chosen vessel who God used to go forth and demonstrate the gospel of Jesus Christ.

Peter was obedient and went to the house of Cornelius. Peter, like Elijah was instructed to "go" to the home of a Gentile. This was the opposite of what they had been taught in their Jewish upbringing. The place called "there" may not be the place you would naturally choose to go. Whether it's in Jerusalem, Judea, Samaria, or the utter most part of the earth God has chosen you to **"go"**. The place is where there is a great need for help and hunger for the gospel of the "kingdom" to be shared. A desperately hungry widow and a spiritually hungry centurion both received the blessing from a man of God directed,"commanded to go" to their homes.

Don't be deceived by opposition from Satan. This is just how Satan works. He tries to get you (us) to deny the reality of what we see from God about our kingdom assignment (destiny). He deceives and manipulates, so doubt and fear can come in to keep you from going on that assignment God has called you to do. The dreams and visions of when and where God is leading you in your assignment is his ultimate goal to destroy which involves purpose and destiny. Your dream is who you are, don't let anyone come in and take your dream. Satan may try to delay, hinder, sift, oppose, and confuse, but the moment of your breakthrough must come. Although the hands of the clock move almost imperceptibly, the moment inevitably arrives when the clock strikes the hour.

Joseph didn't loose sight of the dream. He faced all types of opposition from family members and outsiders. Joseph was faithful to God in doing his assignment. Even if his dream had the jealousy of his brothers, being sold, the lies of Potiphar's wife, the putting him in a pit, going to prison, yet all for the purpose of fulfilling the dream to save and bless his family and a nation. Remember, following Jesus and doing what God has called you to do is not popular or comfortable. Christianity is not popular. If you want to do things that is comfortable don't follow Jesus because its all about having a relationship with him and seeking the **"kingdom" at all cost.**

The Lord protects all those who love, him, but he destroys the wicked.
Psalm 145:20

The principle is so beautifully illustrated in the lives of Joash and Paul. Little Joash, at only seven years of age, was defenseless against the ruthless Queen Athaliah. "Joash and his nurse remained hidden in the Temple of the Lord for six years while Athaliah ruled over the land" (II Kings 11:3). Only the Lord could have kept him from crying at the wrong moment or being seen by someone who was friends to the queen. Athaliah finally met her death, the Lord fulfilling His promise to destroy the wicked. Paul faced great danger from the Jews at Corinth, "' One night the Lord spoke to Paul in a vision and told him," *Don't be afraid! Speak out! Don't be silent! For I am with you, no one will harm you because many people here in this city belong to me"* (Acts 18:9-10). The Jews efforts to bring legal action against Paul ended in their being thrown out of court in one moment of time. Satan makes you think the end is here, the worst has come, and the game is lost, but remember it's not over until the Lord says it's over. The Lord is watching over you as He leads you in your assignment for the "kingdom" purpose.

Scriptures: Psalm 34:18; Psalm 134:1-3; Isaiah 40:1; Proverbs 18:10 John 17:23; Romans 8:31; I Corinthians 1:3-7;

Esther is another example of an orphan girl who was willing to face opposition to do her assignment. Along with guidance and encouragement from Mordecai, Esther was determined to go to the king on behalf of the Jews. Even if it meant that she would "perish" it didn't stop her from fulfilling her destiny.

In spite of what King Ahasuerus would do or the plan that Haman had set into action that threatened to annihilate all of the Jewish people it was never beyond God's control. His dreadful intentions were impossible while God was protecting His people. Although many try to justify their position mainly by stressing that God's name is never mentioned in the Book of Esther, this should not be a reason for concern, since the main purpose of the book is clearly providential of God and His care for His people. Esther became Queen, the king honored Mordecai who saved the King's life, and a Jewish nation was saved all because of obedience to God. The same very plot that Haman went with to King Ahasuerus, he succumbed to that very destruction of death. God will take care of His own!

Beware of the opposition you face in the church, and other believers you come in contact with who are not going where God is taking you. Your assignment was given to you from God and you don't need anyone to affirm or validate what God has called/chosen you to do. Agreement is the key. Whether the assignment is locally, from state-to-state, or even internationally God wants you to be connected with the right people. Don't allow opposition to come in through people who have attached themselves to the assignment God has called you to.

Those who carry the spirits of control, manipulation, fear/doubt, and all about self, **fear not** they are under your feet. These spirits have been trained to come in to discourage, disrupt, destroy, and stop what God has commanded you to do. Remember, if they can't control it they will try to destroy it, but be reassured they can't destroy the power and works of the Holy Spirit. You want someone that God has sent to walk with you and people who are on fire with a purpose and passion for the kingdom of God. Regardless, if it's one or a few you all must be on one accord in unity. **Just go!**

Jesus on the other hand is in the business of opening our minds, reminds us what God has shown us is true and it will come to pass. God gives us the boldness, confidence, and revelation when we seek and speak the Word of the Lord. When the enemy knows you have this he tries to bring fear to stop you and your destiny. You've been **"commanded to go"**. Remember you have a kingdom mind-set; Satan can't stop you from fulfilling the assignment God has told you to do. The scripture in Luke 24:45 remind us that for the eleven disciples; He "opened their minds to understand". When Jesus opens our eyes we begin to recognize and understand that God has given us authority (power) to do everything he has ordained for our lives. Why not ask the Lord give me eyes to see! Just as you've faced opposition from those in the church, as well as outside of the church you will sometimes face opposition from those in your own family.

Handling opposition is difficult, especially if the opposition is from those you love. Jesus faced opposition continually even from those in His own family who said, "He's out of his mind" (Mark 3:21). In addition, Jesus also faced opposition from the teachers of the Law who remarked, "he possessed by Satan" verse 22. David gave the best prescription for handling opposition. First, he said to trust in the Lord, never believe that a problem is yours. Just relax as a baby would in the arms of its mother. Second, David said to delight in the Lord. Keep your focus on the delightful relation between you and God. Never allow the devil to steal your joy and the sense that all is well. Third, he said to "commit everything you do to the Lord" (Psalm 37:5), commit means "to roll". Just shift the weight of opposition from your shoulders onto the shoulders of God. He is more than able to carry it. David said in Psalm 37:7 to "be still". How quickly we want to take matters in our own hands when opposition rises up against us when doing our assignments. We think it is better to "fight fire with fire". Christian believers have to learn to discipline themselves to wait on the Lord and He will to fight the battle for us. Trust, delight, commit, and be still, and in the end you will see that the battle belongs to the Lord.

Cross References: I Samuel 15:22; Psalm 37:1-11; Psalm 55:22-23; Proverbs 16:3 Mark 3:7-30; I Peter 5:7

Some believers may think the gospel is difficult and the kingdom is controversial because of the opposition they face. Yes! Let's put this into perspective because Jesus call to follow involves speaking out against everyone and everything that hinders God's vision for the world and advancing His kingdom here on earth. Christian believers face challenges but God's word is there, the "good news" which is a word of exhortation and comfort. We must embrace God's vision for the world which will put us at odds with the values and character of a dark world that is determined on promoting and organizing itself around the very things that are opposed to God. The church (body of Christ) has a mission to bring forth the "kingdom" here on earth. Our assignment is to "go" into all the world, "go" in every system in the world to share the gospel of Jesus Christ and make disciples.

There are so many examples we find in the bible about individuals who went to do their "kingdom assignment" for which God had purpose and ordained them to do. Regardless, of where they came from or who they were there was a purpose to "go". Here is a list of some examples:

*Abram went from his kindred and was blessed, now Abraham is the father of nations
*Joseph went from the pit to the palace
*Moses went to Pharoah and spoke what God instructed him to do.
*Joshua went to Jericho, walls came down
*Deborah, a prophetess went to tend her father's sheep.
*Esther went to the king, found favor and the Jewish nation was saved.
*Ruth went and gleaned in the field and married Boaz.
*David went and sleuthed Goliath.
*Ezekiel went to voice the prophetic words of God.
*Isaiah went to voice the prophetic messages from God.
*Jeremiah went as an appointed prophet before his birth.
*Matthew, Mark, Luke, and John went spreading the "gospel" of Jesus Christ.
*Peter and Paul went preaching sermons to those that which was lost.

*John the Baptist went crying in the wilderness saying, "repent" for the kingdom of God is at hand. (salvation)
*Jesus went preaching, teaching, healing, and then would **"go"** and give His life for the sins of the world, the ultimate sacrifice on the cross and was resurrected with **all** power and might. Jesus Saves!

The Blood Speaks

Christian believers often sing about the **power of the blood**, but yet most believers seldom use or enter into the power. Most don't even know or can comprehend the great significance of the **"blood"** of Jesus. We often hear time after time over and over again how some believers "plead the blood" of Jesus, but few can explain its great power and benefits. Yes, you have the power just speak the "blood"! Have you ever asked another believer what the power of the blood means? Do you know yourself what the blood of Jesus Christ means in your life? Even Satan understands the power of the **"blood of Jesus"** and he has done everything possible to blind and deceive Christians from this truth. Remember, our inheritance of forgiveness of sin and eternal life is brought about through the power of the shed blood of Jesus Christ.

John the Baptist announced His coming, he spoke of Him (Jesus) as filling a dual office (role), as "the **LAMB OF GOD** that taketh away the sins of the world" and then as "the one who would baptize with the Holy Spirit". The outpouring of the Blood of the Lamb of God took place first, before the outpouring of the Spirit could be bestowed. The Blood of Jesus Christ, the act of the Atonement for our sins is in the shedding of the blood in Jesus Christ's death. The "blood speaks" and it has never lost its power and never will. The atonement was for man to be reconciled back to God. The blood of Jesus Christ is His sacrificial death. (Ephesians 1:7; Colossians 1:14; and Revelation 1:5.)

The first biblical reference to the "blood" is the sprinkling of the blood in Exodus Chapter 12:22. There is also a sprinkling of blood mentioned in Exodus 24:1-11. In these passages of scripture, God made a covenant agreement with Israel. He promised, "If you will obey my words, I will be a God to you, and you will be my people. As Christian believers we have a covenant with God our Father and we have benefits of the "blood of Jesus". The power is in the blood which involves (1) the blood saves, (2) the blood heals, (3) the blood delivers, (4) the blood cleanse and sanctifies us, (5) the blood redeems us from sickness, death and the curse of the law, (6) the blood sets us free and makes us whole and (7) the blood destroys the power of Satan. These are just some of the benefits we have as children of God to know as we "go" while doing our "kingdom" assignments.

As you "go" on your kingdom assignment from God never ever forget that the **"Blood Speaks"**. You can't do anything for God without the power of the blood. You can't come by any other name, only by the "blood of Jesus". God has given us the power and authority to **"speak the blood"** of

Jesus. Demons tremble at the very name of Jesus when you speak. We are warriors...blood bought, blood saved, more than conquerors through JESUS CHRIST. There is nothing more powerful than the **"Blood of Jesus"**. It's what we need in every spiritual battle, challenges we face, trials, temptations, and definitely for the times we're living in. Pleading the blood of Jesus when we speak is the scriptural way of "enforcing the victory of Calvary".

We have heard often times in church or just simply from one believer to another the statement: What can wash away my sins nothing but the "blood" of Jesus or what can make me whole again nothing but the "blood" of Jesus. These phrases of chorus have been sung over and over again throughout time and so many still don't realize the significance of the blood of Jesus Christ. The blood in Jesus was real. He had to die on a certain day and time, fulfilled the plan as the "Passover Lamb". The blood of Jesus Christ was sacrificial, His death given to mankind for our sins. Don't forget! He was given as a "lamb" on a specific day and time for a specific purpose, and prophesy was fulfilled. He humbled himself and became obedient to the part of death, even the death on the cross. "How much more shall the blood of Christ, who through the eternal Spirit offered himself without spot to God, purge your conscience from dead works to serve the living God" (Hebrews 9:14).

Jesus **"blood"** was for the cleansing and forgiveness of sins. I Peter 1:18-19 states: "For you know that it was not with perishable things such as silver or gold that you were redeemed but with the precious **blood of Christ**". The bible also states in Ephesians 1:7-8 that "In him we have redemption through His blood, the forgiveness of sins, in accordance with the riches of God's grace that He lavished on us".

Let's take another look at the list below about what the **"blood"** does for those that are **believers and saved.**

- Acts 20:28..............You are bought with it.
- Romans 5:9............You are justified with it.
- Ephesians 1:7.........Redemption through it.
- Colossians 1:20......Peace with God through it.
- Hebrews 9:22........No forgiveness without it.
- Revelation 1:5.......You are freed from sin by it.
- Revelation 12:11....You overcome the accuser with it.
- Revelation 14:12.....You are made holy by it.

The blood of Jesus Christ is our weapon to destroy the very kingdom of hell and as Christian believers be ready and available to "go" on what ever assignment God has called you to. Jesus has given us the power because the **"blood speaks"**.

<u>Chapter 5 Questions and Exercises</u>

1. Do you know what your "kingdom assignment" is?

2. List 8 of the character traits a "leader' should have mentioned in this Chapter.

    _____

    _____

3. What is the Greek word for "light" and "darkness"? Where in I John Chapter 1 does he teach us about light and darkness? Write the verses down.

4. Jesus said: "I Am the _____ of the world.

5. List the 7 scriptures mentioned in the Romans Road to Salvation below.

    _____

    _____

    _____

6. What book of the bible states: "Can two walk together, except they be agreed?" Write the scripture down from memory.

7. List several bible characters stated in this Chapter that had a purpose to 'go' and fulfill their destiny.

    _____

    _____

8. In Acts Chapter 1:8 what was the "command" that Jesus repeated to the disciples?

9. What is the Greek word for "go" and what does it mean by definition?

10. List 3 scriptures that refers to the "blood of Jesus Christ" in this Chapter.

    _____

    _____

"Ask Jesus to save you now and have eternal life". Dear Lord Jesus I repent of my sins; Come into my heart and save me. I believe Romans 10:9 which says: That if thou shalt confess with thy mouth the Lord Jesus, and shalt believe in thine heart that God hath raised him from the dead, thou <u>shalt be saved.</u> "For whosoever shall call upon the name of the <u>Lord shall be saved</u> (Romans 10:13).

CHAPTER 6

Kingdom Wealth

Let him labor working with his hands the thing which is good, that he may have to
give to him that needed.
Ephesians 4:28

When we see the word wealth the first thing that comes in our mind is money. The word wealth can be defined as: abundance of valuable material, possessions, or resources, or abundant supply quotes the Merriam Webster Dictionary. There are many different definitions on the word wealth which mainly people relates to money only. When we seek God for the kingdom (Matthew 6:33) the wealth will follow, so we are able to do our kingdom assignments. Stop seeking God for stuff! Have you ever ask God for the wealth of wisdom, fruits of the spirit, forgiveness, discernment, knowledge, or how to renew your mind? Why not pursue and seek those riches that are eternal and will last? The material things will fade and rust away (Matthew 6:19-21). These things are temporal. God will always provide for us every resource of what is needed to fulfill His kingdom purpose for the world for His glory. God wants us to have wisdom in using kingdom wealth. Remember the **kingdom** is in you! (Deuteronomy 8:18)

From the biblical perspective of wealth we can take a good lesson from Solomon. The anointed and proclaimed King Solomon, who in his early life was bright with promise and it was God's purpose that he should go forth to do what he was called and chosen to do. For many years Solomon's life was marked with devotion to God, with uprightness, principles, and obedience to God's command. He managed and directed the business matters wisely which was connected to the kingdom. Even with all his wealth Solomon realized that wisdom was far greater than any other thing, which would lead him in how to use God's wealth.

Solomon desired wisdom to lead God's people, and the Lord granted it. He also granted him great wealth and power even though Solomon did not ask for those things. During his time he reigned as king in righteousness, when he followed God's leadership the kingdom of Israel reached its greatest strength and her borders expanded further. Yes! Solomon did make some wrong choices in his life, but yet the wisdom that Solomon desired above riches, honor, or long life, God gave him. His petition for a changed mind, a large heart, and a tender spirit was granted. Solomon wisdom and understanding was exceedingly much. It excelled the wisdom of all the children of the east country, and all the wisdom of Egypt. For he was wiser than all men; and his fame was in all nations round about. (I Kings 4:29-31)

I Timothy 6:10 says: "for the love of money is the root of all evil; which while some coveted after, they have erred from faith, and pierced themselves through with many sorrows". The love of money! If you have made money and things your gods, would you really be able to give up the wealth for the kingdom cause. Christian believers please don't hesitate to use God's wealth for the plan and purpose of His kingdom.

Wealth from the world perspective is based on how much, how many, and more and more is better. This becomes an issue when things such as money, houses, cars, jewelry, and people now have become your little gods. One of the main questions you should ask is the wealth/money your own? No! God has given us everything we have in spite of how we use it. Wealth that is earned or given to us in an honest matter is from God. We are simply stewards of it, and we will answer to God (give an account) for how we used the wealth He gave us. Seeing wealth/money through a kingdom mind-set will help us faithfully steward and manage our money according to principles from the bible.

We will be freely able to bless, give, serve, and help others based on the wealth given to us by God. The focus should be on Christ, and as we focus on Him all our needs will be supplied (Matthew 6:33; Philippians 4:19). Some believers may never quite understand why there are those who have prosperity and those who live in poverty but in all things God is sovereign. Both poverty and prosperity can be a curse and a blessing depending on how your situation is received. The bible teaches us in Matthew 26:11, *"For ye have the poor always with you"* (KJV).

Wealth shouldn't be squandered on earthly pleasure, but should be used to advance God's kingdom. Wealth should be used for God's plan and purpose for the whole earth. God blesses and gives wealth in order to help establish and keep a community that brings honor to His name.

Kingdom Wealth and Parables

Jesus had lots to say about money; about how wealth is obtained and how it should be used and shared. He does not condemn the rich/wealthy but those who gain or maintain their riches through unjust means such as theft, exploitation, greed, stinginess, and especially violence. In the parables of the Unjust Steward (Luke 16:1-13), Lost Coin (Luke 15:8-10), and Lost Son (Luke 15:11-32) Jesus clearly was establishing a Mosaic standard among the people. Luke also gives us an example in the parable of the Rich Man and Lazarus (Luke 16:19-31 KJV), forgiveness of both the repentant tax collectors and the repentant sinner will help accomplish the plan and purpose of God.

As believers and children of God we must operate God's wealth according to his plan. This is very important and what Jesus was presenting to them in parables concerning wealth. There is an issue at hand, with wealth and how it's used and for what purpose. Jesus is saying the people of this world know how to build their personal kingdom, but when it comes to God's people they do not seem to be wise. Many in the body of Christ use wealth to build their own ministries, their own churches and often they do not use the wealth to build the kingdom of God. There have been many in leadership that use the money for putting on elaborate programs, plays, unnecessary spending on church décor to compete with other ministries, and other things just for their own "selfish" purposes.

We must ask these questions: Does God care about the size of a particular church? Does it really matter if you have 50, or 5,000 members? Is it really about your carpet, your cameras, or decorative pulpit? When we're talking about the kingdom of God, kingdom wealth will take care of the needs of God's people. God cares about souls being **saved, feeding the poor, healing the sick, teaching the word, clothing the naked, finding shelter for the homeless, loving the hopeless,** and doing just what Jesus would do and so much more. Kingdom wealth is great to have and we should have it but never ever forget that this wealth is to bring life and hope to others. If we are building people in the kingdom of God then God will bring the buildings and resources to do this. Whether the body of Christ is big or small, if the mind-set of the believer has not changed to a kingdom mind-set they will never be able to effectively change the world nor will they be able to see from a kingdom viewpoint. Remember the kingdom is about changing lives!

Today in this 21st Century we as believers have witnessed how many have fallen because of their wealth/money. Many in the church just as well as those of this world is going through financial problems. America and the world have now experienced the collapse of the world system because of greed, corruption, manipulation, fraud, and cover-ups on every end, where wealth has been misused and funds have been misappropriated. America and the world have been exposed for what they really have been doing. Many feel there is no need for God in their lives because they are self-sufficient and rely only on themselves. I'm referring to the God we serve who raised Jesus from the dead our Lord and Savior. When God is taken out of the equation this is the effect of what happens. The world system has been turned inside out and upside down. The world in such a chaotic state, where their housing market have fallen, their banks have fallen, school systems have declined, automobile industry have taken a huge dive, insurance companies went belly-up, and so many other industries have followed and filed bankruptcy. The money isn't worth the paper it's printed on.

Many believers have fallen for the trap of gaining more wealth and using it to pursue things that doesn't benefit the kingdom of God. James Chapter 5:1-8 teaches believers about the warnings to the rich and yet many believers have done exactly the same what James warns against. Leaders have sacrificed their marriage, sacrificed their children, and health to get wealth (Exodus 20:3). There are many in trouble today because they have allowed their wealth to become their idol. Some believers are not wise in spending and handling wealth, it should be treated as a servant instead of a master (Proverbs 21:20). As children of the kingdom we are for God. Yes! We are all God's creation but not all His children. You are only a child of God when you accept **Jesus as your Savior and Lord** (Romans 10:9, 13). We don't own anything here, not even ourselves.

There are also many churches who have succumbed to this same fate because of how they have used God's house to advance their own little "kingdom". Christian believers should never use the world way or methods to build a solid foundation in having kingdom wealth. Our motives for wealth should not be based upon why and how we do things. The wealth is not to intimidate others, ridicule, defy, challenge those less fortunate. The world builds their kingdom based on themselves. **It's all about I! You can never make kingdom wealth about you, it's always about others**. What ever God has given us to use for his kingdom we should do exactly that. Jesus, speaks in Luke Chapter 19:13, *"and he called his ten servants, and delivered them ten pounds, and said unto them, **Occupy till I come***.

Kingdom wealth operates on a unique but foundational purpose which is referred to as God's economy. Just like Jesus explained all dimensions of God's kingdom it starts like a grain of mustard seed, small and innocuous, but potent and unstoppable in its growth. Christian believers must remember when we look at God's economy **it defines human logic and reasoning** and is totally different from the power structure commonly accepted by the world standards as the foundation of wealth. Genesis Chapter 26:1-3; 12-13 says: "There was a famine in the land and the Lord appeared to Isaac and said: Dwell in this land, and I will be with you and bless you and perform the oath which I swore to Abraham your father". So Isaac sowed in that land, and reaped in the same year a hundred-fold; and the Lord blessed him. So he began to prosper, and continued prospering until he became very prosperous".

Kingdom wealth is what God uses to establish His Covenant with His children. For example Isaac obedience along with faith sowed during a famine, because God told him to and he prospered. What ever God tells us to do concerning His "kingdom", He is always involved in the center of the assignment, the expectation of the outcome exceeds what ever you and I might hope for or accomplish in the natural realm.

Jesus taught parables in Luke Chapter 19:11-27 and Matthew 25:14-30 concerning one's responsibility. In contrast between these parables: The nobleman gave equally one pound to each person, but in the parable of the talents in Matthew he bestowed unequal endowments. . He expected the proper yield proportionate to his endowment. This is in confirmation of what Paul stated in I Corinthians 4:7 "and what hast thou that thou didst not receive? Now if thou didst receive it, why dost thou glory as if thou hadst not received it?" All things have been received from God. No one can say that he has received nothing. No matter how much or how little one has, it must always be remembered that it comes from God, and that he/she is responsible to Him for the way it is used. Believers are to be honest in doing business with others, have integrity, and hold the same standards that Jesus would have. Remember the wealth that God gives us must be able to work for the kingdom. Again, be very careful that you don't allow the money to master you; it should be a servant for God's people.

The times we are living in now have more than ever given one of the greatest opportunities for believers to use our resources to proclaim and advance the "kingdom of God'. The bible is full of examples of godly men who used there wealth to spread the truth—men like Joseph, David, Solomon, Daniel and so on. God wants us to use our talents, skills, gifts and experience to create products and services to generate profits which will expand His kingdom here on earth. The concept and issues of kingdom wealth may be hard for some to grasp, but it is very significant and essential to understand, along with comprehending the dynamics of a wealth transfer.

Wealth Transfer

Solomon teaches us in Proverbs 13:22 (ASV), "A good man leaveth an inheritance to his children's children: and the wealth of the sinner is laid up for the righteous. There has been a paradigm shift in the spiritual realm to the earthly realm. This is a power shift that is leading and driving a mature (remnant) body, God's given perspective and purpose is to guide their hearts/steps to advance His kingdom here on earth. The focal point and purpose for "kingdom wealth" will be God's agenda. It's about restoration, redemption, dominion, and authority.

Cross References: Ezra 9:12; Job 27:16-17; Psalm 37:25; Proverbs 28:8; Ecclesiastes 2:26

Now Is the Time! The **"remnant"** kingdom builders have been positioned and poised to be transitioned for the powerful new paradigm shift from the spiritual (heavenly) realm to the earthly realm. This paradigm shift will bring forth the emerging groups of forerunners, pace setters, trail blazers, and nation's changers to destroy, eradicate, and annihilate every kingdom systems of darkness in this world through the anointing/power **by the blood of Jesus**. Remember **the blood speaks**! This remnant of kingdom builders should be distinguished from other believers who simply might be described as successful business people. The "remnant" called and chosen by God for such a time as this to advance the "kingdom of God" by any means necessary.

These "Anointed leaders" will serve in key roles to accomplish and fulfill God's purpose here on earth which is to bring forth redemption, restoration, and authority. Leaders are sharing the gospel of Jesus Christ, helping the poor, homeless, healing the lame, deaf, blind, and have the power to raise the dead. The remnant who God has given **"favor"** are men and woman of influence. The remnant who God has called and chosen will have a supernatural flow of money and wealth out of the hands of the sinner (wicked) given into their hands by God's doing to advance His "kingdom" here in the earth realm. This wealth has a mission and a "kingdom assignment" in the earth **to go into all the world and establish God's Covenant.**

Yes, without a doubt the transfer of the wealth from the world (sinner, wicked) to God's children for His kingdom will be put in our hands (the righteous) to build and promote His kingdom here in the earth realm. Yes! Let the Spirit in me prophesy to you that there has been a paradigm shift and the old is out and the new has arrived. The Holy Spirit gave me this in 2009 before we entered into 2010 that you can't put new wine into old wine skin. This prophetic word was confirmed on several occasions even in the house of God that I attend. God is speaking through His Prophets/ Prophetess and to those who will hear what the Spirit is saying to the church. There is nothing or no one that can stop this wealth transfer that has manifested in the earth realm to put in the hands of God's chosen ones. The very depths of hell can't stop this. God is advancing His "kingdom" now here on earth and putting His "remnant" in position for proper alignment to receive the wealth.

The "remnant" kingdom builders are very driven, direct, motivated, innovative, bold, and creative. They build in a manner that advances the kingdom of God. Kingdom builders represent the essence of Jesus teaching on the parable of the talents found in Matthew Chapter 25 verses 14-30 and Luke Chapter 19 verses 11-27. Hebrews 11:6 tells us that "for he that cometh to God must first believe that he is, and that he is a rewarder of them that diligently seek him. We must believe that God's economy operates by faith and He has the power to transfer the wealth of the sinner (wicked) to the righteous. As Christian believers our kingdom mind-set releases a Spirit of building, creating, and innovating instead of being mediocre or stuck in doubt and fear. A strategic plan to use the wealth that has been transferred from the sinners (wicked) hands into the righteous hands so spiritual riches, community riches, and economic riches can be used to help God's people. God has given us this wealth transfer to build and advance His kingdom here on earth as we endure and stand boldly as ambassadors of Jesus Christ our Lord and Savior. We are to exercise the fruits through the truth of God's word and what it says. Proverbs 11:30 states: **"The fruit of the righteous is a tree of life; and he that winneth souls is wise.**

Ephesians 4:11 teaches us the five-fold ministry of Apostles, Prophets, Evangelists, Pastors, and Teachers, which **Now Is the Time** these gifts should be operating in such a greater magnitude, which will manifest the power of God through the Holy Spirit moving stronger in the body and the world (communities) in the days before us. These ministries understand the dynamics of being "**kingdom-connectors**" along with other lay ministries so the interaction between the spiritual, community, (earth realm) and God's kingdom riches can come together and be used for the advancement of His kingdom here on earth.

Here are some examples of biblical transfers of great wealth, God getting the wealth out of the hands of the wicked and into the hands of His children.

Joseph in Egypt through seven years of great prosperity followed by seven years of famine, the wealth of Egypt and the world was brought into the hands of Joseph. (Genesis 47:13-26)

Israel in its exodus from Egypt after 10 plagues from God, the Egyptians gave Israel all its money just to get rid of them. (Exodus 7-12)(Exodus 12:35)

King Solomon accumulated so much gold, and silver was not even counted. (I Kings 10:13-27) (II Chronicles 9:13-27) and God has said that He will build again tabernacle of David. (Acts 15:16); (Amos 9:11); (Isaiah 16:5); which included wealth as well as worship.

II Kings Chapter 7 (four lepers and the army of Syria) God causes the army of Syria to hear a noise of horses, chariots and a host which caused the army to flee and leave behind enough wealth to bring Israel out of famine and an economic depression in one day.

II Chronicles 20:1-25 Judah is delivered from the armies of 3 nations after God's people worshipped Him on the battlefield, God supernaturally caused the armies against Judah to destroy one another, and it took , and took, 3 days to carry away all the spoils.

The transfer of the wealth from the sinner (wicked) is manifesting in the earth realm so the "**remnant**" that God has called and chosen to accomplish and complete their assignments here on earth to advance and promote His "**kingdom**" will come to pass. Watch and Pray! **Now Is the Time!** The glory of the Lord will shine on earth. Isaiah Chapter 60 verses 1-2 speaks about the "Future Glory of Zion" and says: "Arise shine for thy light is come; and the glory of the Lord is risen upon thee. For, behold, the darkness shall cover the earth, and gross darkness the people: **but the Lord shall arise upon thee**, **and his glory shall be seen upon thee**. (KJV)

Wealth that Serves

There are so many ways that we can use wealth to serve others. This is what God has called us to do as kingdom people. The wealth/money that God has bestowed on us is for the purpose of His kingdom. When we make it **a priority to let the wealth we have be a servant to others** it is without doubt God will take care of us. Christian believers are to be good stewards over everything God has given us. In Luke Chapter 12:41:44, Peter said unto the Lord, speakest thou this parable unto us, or even to all? "And the Lord said, *who then is that faithful and wise steward, who his lord* *shall make ruler over his household, to give them their portion of meat in due season. Blesses is that servant whom his lord when he cometh shall find so doing. Of a truth I say unto you, that he will make him ruler over all that he hath".*

Christian believers must be very careful that money doesn't consume them. Don't let money master you! Let it be a servant for God's kingdom. Don't worry about having a bigger salary, bigger house, cars, or other consuming things the world dictates as a must have because the more you get, the more your flesh will desire. Don't misinterpret what I'm teaching here! God is not against people having money! It's what you do with it that matters. Money must be kept in proper balance, and be not deceived by money. The deceitfulness of riches will be used by Satan to destroy you. Matthew Chapter 13:22 quotes Jesus saying, *"He also that received seed among the thorns is he that heareth the word; and the care of this world, and the deceitfulness of riches, choke the word, and he becometh unfruitful".* Don't believe the lie that money is stable. If God would bless you right now with $10 billion dollars what would you do with it? Would you ever possibly consider doing anything with that amount of wealth to serve His people, promote or advance His kingdom?

Do you really believe that money will satisfy your soul? The bible says in Matthew Chapter 16:26 which Jesus speaks: *"For what is a man profited, if he shall gain the whole world, and lose his own soul? Or what shall give in exchange for his soul?"* Do you believe that wealth will solve all your problems? A rich man/woman dying with cancer still needs a **Savior.** Can you recall the last time you had an opportunity to serve others with the wealth/money God has blessed you with? Why not take an inventory of all your assets and see how much you have? Some are not as fortunate as others, but those who seem to **have less is willing to do whatever they can to serve God's kingdom.** Let your heart guide your wealth! Is your wealth for the kingdom cause? Don't love money; be satisfied with what you have. For God has said. "I will never fail you. I will never abandon you" (Hebrews 13:5).

Contentment lies not in how much money or things we have or what we call ours, but only in Jesus. Envy causes one to look horizontally at what others have so we are never satisfied.

Matthew Chapter 6:19-21 paints a clear picture in this text of scriptures which Jesus states: *"Lay not up for yourselves treasures upon earth, where moth and rust doth corrupt, and where thieves break through and steal. But lay up for yourselves treasures in heaven, where neither moth nor rust doth corrupt, and where thieves do not break through nor steal. But where your treasure is, there will your heart be also"* (KJV). Are you honoring God with your wealth? Will you be a good steward over the wealth/money when God gives it to you?

Cross References: Luke 9:25; Job 2:4; Job 27:8; Luke 12:16-21; 16:19-25; Psalm 49:6-8 Mark 8:36-37

God wants to bless you so you are able to use whatever He has given you for the kingdom. When the priority of God is put first God will take care of you and your household. The scripture says in II Corinthians 5: 20, "We are therefore Christ's ambassadors, as though God were making His appeal through us". As a believer, God wants to do His work on the earth through you. You are His ambassador or representative. You have been given authority and power. It's easy to get focused on the natural realm and all the things that you want and have the wealth to buy them, but do you realize that you are equipped to be somebody else's miracle. I encourage you to look for ways to be a blessing to someone else. When you pour into others and help meet their needs, God will make sure that others pour into you (Luke 6:38 KJV).

Luke Chapter 16:1-13 gives another example through this parable what Jesus was teaching us on how to be good managers and disciples. In the parable he teaches how to be fruitful in stewardship of material wealth. The parable presents a very wise shrewd man. He is quite dishonest, but he is also intelligent and effective. He knows what he wants and how to get it. This teaches us an example of one being focused, intelligent, and proactive in regards to stewardship.

Jesus teaches us that just as this unrighteous man needed to be shrewd or wise, so does the righteous need to be shrewd and wise. For the people of the world are shrewder in dealing with their own kind than are the people of the **light**. In other words, people who are not Jesus disciples are usually more effective in their use of worldly wealth than Jesus disciples.

Matthew Chapter 6:21 Jesus sates: *"For where your treasure is, there will your heart be also"*. The people of this world have something in their heart which is set on fame or power. That is their treasure, so they pursue it with their whole being. They are willing to use whatever wealth at their disposal to pursue that goal. They are focused and intelligent like the man in the parable. This is why Jesus gives us specific direction on how to use wealth. I tell you, use worldly wealth to gain friends for yourselves, so that when it is gone, you will be welcomed into eternal dwellings. We are to use worldly wealth! We can't waste it or let it just sit there idle. We are to put it to good use, the use for which God intended it. Just as the crooked manager did, Jesus says to use the wealth to make friends. God wants us to use our wealth to serve others and bring them into the kingdom. That is how we serve, love, and honor God.

Is your commitment to wealth costing you more than what your commitment to God cost you? Are you willing to pay the price to gain wealth than pay the price to gain something worth while in the end (eternal treasures)? Let's take a look again at the story in Luke Chapter 15 verses 11-18. There were two sons and the younger son said to his father give me my portion, so the father divided it between the two. After a few days the younger son took all his wealth and journey to another country. He spent everything he had to fulfill his fleshy desires not concerned about using the wealth to help others. Just as he was willing to leave his father and home so many believers have done the same and are willing to leave God and their church family just because of how they have accumulated much wealth. They choose to believe that their wealth is all they need and can buy or do everything they desire. After, he squandered and wasted all his money in reckless living a severe famine spread over that country, and he was left without a thing.

The younger son went to work for one of the citizens of that country, who sent him into the fields to take care of the swine. He would fain have filled his belly with the husks that the swine did eat, and no man gave him anything to eat. When the young man came to himself he realized that his father has many hired servants and have bread enough to spare and here I am about to starve. He got up and went to his father and said father, I have sinned against God, and against you. Christian believers must never forget their Father, (daddy) is waiting for us with open and loving arms. In spite of how you have wasted, squandered, misused, the wealth God has allowed you to be blessed with He wants to forgive you. **Repent!** And ask God to show you how to use the wealth for His **"kingdom"**. Even the younger son had revelation to realize that all that wealth he had was nothing without the Father's love.

Another example is of the prosperous farmer in Luke Chapter 12:16-21 that Jesus spoke: "*He said what shall I do, because I have no room where to bestow my fruits? And he said, This will I do: I will pull down my barns, and build greater; and there will I bestow all my fruits and my goods. And I will say to my soul, Soul, thou hast much goods laid up for many years; take thine ease, eat, drink, and be merry. But God said unto him, Thou fool this night thy soul shall be required of thee; thee: then whose shall those things be, which thou hast provided? So is he that layeth up treasures for himself, and is not rich toward God.*" The farmer was all about I, Me, and Mind. This farmer labeled all about himself and not even the life to come (eternal). He made a decision to keep it all for himself, not anything about God. Barns were over filled and he didn't want to share with others. Remember money is like sea water, many thirst for more, more, and more never satisfied. What ever you hold on to tightly your going to loose it. The prosperous farmer was concerned about his barns, goats, grains and his **soul was lost.** What is the most valuable things in your life? The prosperous farmer reasoned with his self-based on the world ways (system) to get all he can. Remember, the most valuable things in your life or your salvation and the Word of God. This is **eternal!**

Jesus was willing to do what ever it cost. Yes, I want your will to be done, not mine, He replied to the Father. Anything worth sharing is doing the will of the Father. Seek the "kingdom of God"! (Matthew 6:33). Go after it! Chase it! You are the light of the world, go and house somebody, clothe somebody, feed somebody, and then you have showed the love of the gospel. God wants to use you as an example of being blessed. Empower your life to share what wealth He has provided you with as the "kingdom" is advanced. You can't say you love God and hate your brother nor can you say you love God and ignore your brother. **Share the wealth!**

Jesus also taught the parable of the judgment where the king said to those who properly used their wealth. I tell you the truth, whatever you did for one of the least of these brothers of mind you did for me (Matthew 25:40 NIV). When we do that we use worldly wealth to make such friends, we are living by faith in Christ. We must remember our use of worldly wealth does matter to Jesus. In fact it is a test of our faithfulness. Whoever can be trusted with very little can also be trusted with much, and whoever is dishonest with very little will also be dishonest with much. So if you have not been trustworthy in handling worldly wealth, who will trust you with true riches? If you have not been trustworthy with someone else's property, who will give you property of your own? Regardless, of how much wealth God trust us with never forget our treasures are eternal! **Jesus!**

Temporal Wealth vs. Eternal Treasures

Do not set your heart on worldly things, perishable objects. Wealth should be dedicated to building up the "**kingdom of God"** while you are here on earth. Riches are temporal and won't last forever. The writer in Proverbs 23:5 states: Wilt thou set thine eyes upon that which is not? For riches certainly make themselves wings; they fly away as an eagle toward heaven (KJV). The possession of wealth alone does not produce happiness; it is very comfortable to have for the essentials and luxuries of life. The possession of wealth could never satisfy the cravings of the immoral soul of mankind. Instead of looking for wealth to soothe your soul, look to heaven and things that are eternal. We can still read in Luke Chapter 12:16-21 about the parable of the "Prosperous Farmer", we see Jesus teaching in verses 20-21 saying: *"But God said unto him, Thou fool this night thy soul shall be required of thee: then whose shall those things be, which thou hast provided? So is he that layeth up treasures for himself, and is not rich toward God* (KJV).

Regardless, of how the wealth is obtained whether through your labor or in a devious, or dishonest way it is temporal and will never bring the peace and joy that comes through Jesus Christ. When this temporal wealth is obtained through devious and dishonest manners it is not enjoyed because of the fear which robs the human happiness (carnal flesh). Christian believers should not allow fear and doubt to stop us from the joy of helping others here on earth. There is a great difference between temporal wealth and eternal treasures (riches). This is something that many righteous and some unrighteous are aware of.

The *sun rises upon the evil and the good; the Lord sends his rain upon the righteous and upon the unrighteous* (Matthew 5:45), this is manifest before our eyes, and is in our daily lives.

Solomon the wise man, says in Ecclesiastes Chapter 9:11: "I returned and saw under the sun, that the race is not to the swift, nor the battle to the strong, neither yet bread to the wise, nor riches to men of understanding, nor yet favor to men of skill; but time and chance happeneth to them all. Christian believers need to use wisdom in determining what to do with their capabilities concerning using wealth to help others. Furthermore, there is the need to realize that some things should not be done at all, specifically those things which bring reproach to Christ's name. The guiding principle for fulfilling what God has directed believers to do with their wealth should be from the heart.

Paul teaches us the necessity of self-sacrifice is the reason Jesus is so fervent in his preaching on money and why Paul stresses Jesus as a model in his statement on Christian giving in II Corinthians 8:9 (KJV). If we cannot pour our wealth to help others and advance the **"kingdom of God"** then we will surely find ourselves outside, just like the rich young ruler (Matthew 19:21-22). Certain things which people see as important in this life will not be taken with them into eternity. Wealth, prestige, and position will always be left behind. Indeed Christian believers should continue to live for things that are eternal while passing through on earth. The benefits preferred will always be **eternal treasures** (riches) and **"eternal salvation"** not the temporary benefit of wealth.

Matthew 19:16-30 teaches us an example of a rich young man claimed to be righteous and wanted to know what things to do to guarantee eternal life. He thought the kingdom could be earned this way. He was instructed to sell all that he had and follow Christ, which was designed to reveal that the young man treasured his earthly possessions more than eternal treasures. He would rather maintain the life style he had than become a follower of Christ. Are you willing to give up everything you have to follow Christ? Are you willing to use the wealth which is temporary to help others in need and advance the "kingdom of God" here on earth? Jesus teaches his disciples about this parallel claim.

Peter claimed that he and the disciples had left everything to follow Jesus. The disciples might have thought what they were doing deserves God's favor. Jesus rebuked them mildly, but graciously told them of their inheritance in the **"kingdom"** which is far greater then that what they might have earned here on earth; it was by grace from God. These passages are about the teachings of Jesus on entering the "kingdom of heaven". They also teach Christian believers the priorities of this life and the life to come.

As believer's we are to seek eternal riches and use our temporal wealth to help advance God's kingdom in the earth realm through the love of Jesus Christ. We are the hands and feet of Jesus Christ as we live here on earth and go everywhere He sends us. We're to do what is right. Micah Chapter 6:8 says: He hath showed thee, O man what is good: and what doth the Lord require of thee, but to do justly and to have mercy, and to walk humbly with thy God? (KJV)

Jesus said, *"How difficult it would be for those who have wealth to enter the "kingdom of God".* His disciples were astonished, so Jesus went on to raise their astonishment even higher by saying: *"It is easier for a camel to go through the eye of a needle than for a rich person to enter the "kingdom of God".* They responded with disbelief, and said "Then who can be <u>**saved**</u>? Jesus says, *"With men it is impossible, but not with God: for all things are possible"* (Mark 10:23-27). Jesus also warns in another text of scripture that the word of God which is meant to give us life can be choked off from any effectiveness by riches. He says it's like a seed that grows up among thorns that choke it to death:

"They are those who hear, but as they go on their way they are choked by the riches of life, and their fruit does not matter" (Luke 8:14).

As Christian believers we are salt/light, children of the kingdom. We should not love wealth as the world does. Remember, what Matthew 6:19 says: *"Do not lay up for yourselves treasures on earth, where thieves break in and steal, but lay up for yourselves treasures in heaven, where neither moth nor rust destroys and where thieves do not break in and steal"*. Believers are not to hoard earthly possessions, the purpose is to have and give others. Ephesians 4:28 quotes; "Let him labor working with his hands that he may have to give to him who is in need". We're to love and help others the way Jesus did, by showing the true message of Jesus through love, compassion, and giving. Hebrew writer tells us to be content with what we have (Hebrews 13:5-6). God will give us everything we need to help others and send others to help us so the "kingdom of God" will be manifested in the earth realm.

Don't love money, be satisfied with what you have and seek the "kingdom" because God knows everything you need. Many pursue the "god" of money, thinking of what it can buy while envying what others have. Envy causes one to look horizontally at what others have so we are never satisfied. Be content! Contentment lies not in how much money or things you have, what is yours, but in who's you are. Contentment invites us to look ultimately at God, when we look in His direction we know that He is enough and will take care of us. The bare truth is that we brought nothing into the world and we can't take anything out of it including money regardless of how much. God knows what is needed in our lives. We must trust Him and not money (wealth). Too often we take our eyes off God and put them on earthly pursuits, with money (wealth) often on top of the list. Money has as incredible power, much like a magnet and more like a "god" than most of us or willing to admit. Money has caused many to draw away from the things that are **eternal** and life-filling. Always be on your guard with money. Remember don't let money master you, let it be a "servant for the kingdom of God". The heart can only love one God which is eternal not the little gods of this world. When we choose to love God we will discover the marvelous benefits of His "kingdom". You will learn that money can never satisfy the heart, and how important it is to keep your focus on God. **He is enough!**

Since God is the ultimate giver and we are created in His likeness, we are to give also. When we give to help others we show the love of Christ and we function in the manner in which we were created, and therefore produce better results in the world. The most important verse in the bible which many of us all know quotes: *"For God so loved the world that He gave ...."* (John 3:16). This is the greatest gift we will ever receive as Christian believers in our life. There is nothing that can be compared to His gift which is Jesus Christ His only begotten Son here on earth. Just as we were given a gift we also must give.

The bible makes it clear if we are following Jesus we can't have our minds occupied with money. God will supply all of our needs according to His riches in glory by Christ Jesus (Philippians 4:19 KJV). We are to do the same to help others with a need. The more and more we give of this temporal wealth it proves that money doesn't control us. We use the wealth to be a servant to others in the earth realm so God can be glorified. The bible states in II Corinthians 8:13-14, "For I mean not that other men be eased, and ye burdened: But by an equality, that now at this time your abundance may be a supply for their want, that their abundance also may be a supply for your want: that there may be equality".

What ever type of wealth we have whether it is spiritual or financial God wants us to share it. We must never forget as believers in the body of Christ that our spiritual wealth will never be temporal; although the financial wealth is temporal we are to share both of them with others to advance the **"kingdom of God"** here on earth. Just as we give to others God will give unto us. Freely we give and freely we'll receive! Remember while we look not at the things which are seen, but at the things which are not seen: for the things which are seen are **temporal**; but the things which are not seen are **eternal** (II Corinthians 4:18 KJV).

Cross References: Psalms 49:6-10; II Corinthians 9:10-14; Luke 12:21; Luke 18:22

Chapter 6 Questions and Exercises

1. Are you using the wealth and resources God has given you to advance "His kingdom" here on earth?

2. Where in the parable does Jesus speak in Luke Chapter 12 about the faithful and wise servant and blessed servant? Write the verses down.

3. 3. In Matthew Chapter 6:33 Jesus said: "But _____ ye first the _____ of God, and his _____: and all these things shall be added unto you.

4. Luke Chapter 12 Jesus teaches the parable about the _____ farmer. Write down the verses on the lines below.

_____

_____

_____

5. When was the last time you did something for the "kingdom of God"? Do you remember the last time you shared the gospel about Jesus Christ to and un-believer?

6. Do you value your wealth (money) more than the word of God? Is Jesus Christ your first priority or your last resort?

7. Have you stored your treasures here on earth or in heaven? Do you live for things that are temporal or for things that are eternal?

8. Write from memory the scripture verse that Jesus says in Matthew 6:21.

_____

_____

9. Solomon teaches us in Proverbs 13:22 the _____ of the sinner is laid up for the just.

10. The bible says what does it profit a man to _____ the whole world and lose their _____.

"Ask Jesus to save you now and have eternal life". Dear Lord Jesus I repent of my sins: Come into my heart and save me. I believe Romans 10:9 which says: That if thou shalt confess

with thy mouth the <u>Lord Jesus,</u> and shalt believe in thine heart that God hath raised from the dead, thou <u>shalt be saved.</u> "For whosoever shall call upon the name of the <u>Lord shall be saved</u> Romans 10:13.

STUDY GUIDE OF SCRIPTURES LISTED BELOW

Chapter I What Is the Kingdom?

Thine, O Lord, is the greatness and power, and the glory, and the victor, and the majesty: for all that is in the heaven and in the earth, is thine: thine is the kingdom, O Lord, and thou are exalted as head above all.
I Chronicles 29:11

For the kingdom is the Lord's, And he rules over the nation.
Psalm 22:28

The Lord has establishes His throne in heaven, And His kingdom rules over all.
Psalm 103:19

Those who see you will gaze at you, And consider you saying, Is this the man who made the earth terrible, Who shook kingdoms.
Isaiah 14:16

How great are His signs, And how mighty His wonders! His kingdom is and everlasting kingdom, And His dominion is from generation to generation.
Daniel 4:3

And Jesus went about all Galilee, teaching in their synagogues, preaching the gospel of the kingdom, and healing all kinds of sickness and all kinds of disease among the people.
Matthew 4:23

But seek first the kingdom of God and His righteousness, and all these things shall be added to you.
Matthew 6:33

Assuredly, I say to you, among those born of women there has not risen one greater than John the Baptist: but he who is least in the kingdom of heaven is greater than he. And from the days of John the Baptist until now the kingdom of heaven suffers violence, and the violent take it by force.
Matthew 11:11-12

For the kingdom of heaven is like a man traveling to a far country, who called his own servants and delivered his goods to them.
Matthew 25:14

Then Jesus looked around and said to His disciples, "How hard is it for those who have riches to enter the kingdom of God." And the disciples were astonished at His words. But Jesus answered again and said to them. "Children how hard it is for those who trust in riches to enter the kingdom of God." It is easier for a camel to go through the eye of a needle then for a rich man to enter the kingdom of God."
Mark 10:23-25

Do not fear, little flock, for it is your Father's good pleasure to give you the kingdom.
Luke 12:32

Jesus answered, "My kingdom is not of this world. If My kingdom were of this world, My servants would fight, so that I should not be delivered to the Jews, but now My kingdom is not from here.
John 18:36

Then comes the end, when He delivers the kingdom to God the Father, when He puts an end to all rule and all authority and power.
I Corinthians 15:24

He has delivered us from the power of darkness and conveyed us into the kingdom of the Son of His love.
Colossians 1:13

And the Lord will deliver me from, every evil work and preserve me for His heavenly kingdom. To Him, be glory forever and ever. Amen!
II Timothy 4:18

Listen, my beloved, brethren: Has God not chosen the poor of this world to be rich in faith and heirs of the kingdom which He promised to those who love Him?
James 2:5

For so an entrance will be supplied to you abundantly into the everlasting kingdom of our Lord and Savior Jesus Christ.
II Peter 1:11

All Scriptures from the Spirit Filled Life Bible (NKJV)

Chapter II Kingdom Mind-Set

Who hath put wisdom in the inward parts? or who hath given understanding to the heart?
Job 38:36

Thou will keep him in perfect peace; whose mind is stayed on thee: because he trusteth in thee.
Isaiah 26:3

And they come to Jesus, and see him that was possessed with the devil, and had the legion, sitting and clothed, and in his right mind and they were afraid.
Mark 5:15 cf: Luke 8:35

And he answering said, Thou shalt love the Lord thy God with all thy heart, and with all thy soul, and with all thy strength, and with all thy mind, and thy neighbor as thyself.
Luke 10:27

And seek not ye what ye shall eat, or what ye shall drink, neither be ye of doubtful mind.
Luke 12:29

And even as they did not like to retain God in their knowledge, God gave them over to a reprobate mind, to do those things, which are not convenient.
Romans 1:28

Because the carnal mind is enmity against God: for it is not subject to the law of God, neither indeed can be.
Romans 8:7

And be not conformed to this world: but be ye transformed by the renewing of your mind; that ye may prove what is that good and acceptable, and perfect will of God.
Romans 12:2

Be of the same mind, one toward another. Mind not high things, but condescend to men of low estate. Be not wise in your own conceits.
Romans 12:16

For who hath known the mind of the Lord, that he may instruct him? But we have the mind of Christ.
I Corinthians 2:16

For if there be first a willing mind, it is accepted according to that a man hath, and not according to that he hath not.
II Corinthians 8:12

And be renewed in the spirit of your mind.
Ephesians 4:23

Fulfill ye my joy that ye be likeminded, having the same love, being of one accord of one mind.
Philippians 2:2

Let this mind be in you, which was also in Christ Jesus.
Philippians 2:5

And the peace of God, which passeth all understanding, shall keep your hearts and minds through Christ Jesus.
Philippians 4:7

For God hath not given us the spirit of fear: but of power, and of love, and of a sound mind.
II Timothy 1:7

Now as Jannes and Jambres withstood Moses, so do these also resist the truth" men of corrupt minds, reprobate concerning the faith.
II Timothy 3:8

For let not that man think that he shall receive any thing of the Lord. A double minded man is unstable in all his ways.
James 1:7-8

Wherefore gird up the loins; of your mind, be sober and hope to the end for the grace that is to be brought unto you at the revelation of Jesus Christ.
Peter 1:13

All Scriptures from Hebrew –Greek Key Word Study Bible (KJV)

Chapter III Kingdom-Connectors Five Fold Ascension Gifts

A man's gift makes room for him, And brings him before great men.
Proverbs 18:16

Now the names of the twelve **apostles** are these: first Simon, who is called Peter, and Andrew his brother, James the son of Zebedee, and John his brother. Phillip and Bartholomew, Thomas, and Matthew the tax collector, James the son of Alphaeus, and Lebbaeus, whose surname was Thaddaeus, Simon the Cananite, and Judas Iscariot, who also betrayed Him.
Matthew 10:2-3

And when it was day, He called His disciples to Himself; and from them He chose twelve whom He also named **apostles**.
Luke 6:13

But Peter and the other **apostles** answered and said, We ought to obey God rather than men.
Acts 5:29

Paul, a bondservant of Jesus Christ, called to be an **apostle**, separated to the gospel of God.
Romans 1:1

For I speak to you Gentiles, inasmuch as I am an **apostle** to the Gentiles, I magnify my ministry.
Romans 11:13

For I wish that all men were even as I myself, But each one has his own gift from God, one in this manner and another in that.
I Corinthians 7:7

And God has appointed these in the church, first **apostles**, second prophets, third teachers, after that miracles, then gifts of healings, helps, administrations, varieties of tongues.
I Corinthians 12:28

And though I have the gift of prophecy, and understand all mysteries and knowledge, and though I have all faith, so that I could remove mountains, but have not love, I am nothing.
I Corinthians 13:2

For such are false apostles, deceitful workers, transforming themselves into **apostles** of Christ. And no wonder! For Satan himself transforms himself into an angel of light.
II Corinthians 11:13-14

Now, therefore you are no longer strangers and foreigners, but fellow citizens with the saints and members of the household of God, having been built on the foundation of the **apostles** and the prophets, Jesus Christ Himself being the chief cornerstone.
Ephesians 2:19-20

And He Himself gave some to be **apostles**, some prophets, some evangelists, and some pastors and teachers, for the **equipping** of the saints for the work of ministry for the edifying of the body of Christ.
Ephesians 4:11-12

Paul, an **apostle** of Jesus Christ by the will of God, according to the promise of life which is in Christ Jesus.
II Timothy 1:1

Then the Lord came down in the pillar of cloud and stood in the door of the tabernacle, and called Aaron and Miriam, And they both went forward.
Then He said, "Hear now my words: If there is a **prophet** among you, I the Lord, make Myself known to him in a vision: I speak to him in a dream.
Numbers 12:5-6

The Lord your God, will raise up for you a **Prophet** like me from your midst, from your brethren, Him you shall hear.
Deuteronomy 18:15

Then Elijah said to the people, I alone am left a **prophet** of the Lord, but Baal's prophets are four hundred and fifty men.
I Kings 18:22

Now Elijah took his mantle, rolled it up, and struck the water; and it was divide this way and that, so that the two of them crossed over on dry ground. And so it was, when they had crossed over, that Elijah said unto Elisha, "Ask! What I do for you, before I am taken away from you?" Elisha said. "Please let a double portion of your spirit be upon me."
II Kings 2:8-9

Also I heard the voice of the Lord, saying:
"Whom shall I send ,
And who will go for Us?"
Then I said, "Here am I! Send me."
Isaiah 6:8

For unto us a Child is born, Unto us a Son is given: And the government will be upon His shoulder, And His name will be called Wonderful Counselor, Mighty God, Everlasting Father, Prince of Peace.
Isaiah 9:6

"Before I formed you in the womb I knew you; Before you were born I sanctified you: I ordained you a **prophet** to the nations."
Jeremiah 1:5

As for them, whether they hear or whether they refuse-for they are a rebellious house-yet they will know that a **prophet** has been among them.
Ezekiel 2:5

And if the **prophet** is induced to speak anything, I the Lord have to induced that prophet, and I will stretch out My hand against him and destroy him from among, My people Israel.
Ezekiel 14:9

Your fathers, where are they?
And the prophets, do they live forever?
Yet surely My words and My statues,
Which I commanded My servants the prophets,
Did they not overtake your fathers?
Zechariah 1:5-6

Behold I will send you Elijah the **prophet**. Behold the coming of the great and dreadful day of the Lord. And he will turn the hearts of the fathers to the children, And the hearts of the children to their fathers. Lest I come and strike the earth with a curse.
Malachi 4:5-6

So they said to him, "In Bethlehem of Judea, for thus it is written by the prophet:
But you, Bethlehem, in the land of Judah,
Are not the least among the rulers of Judah;
For out of you shall come a Ruler
Who will shepherd My people Israel."
Matthew 2:5-6

Beware of false **prophets**, who come to you in sheep's clothing, but inwardly they are ravenous wolves.
Matthew 7:15

He who receives a **prophet** in the name of a prophet shall receive a prophet's reward. And he who receives a righteous man in the name of a righteous man shall receive a righteous man's reward.
Matthew 10:41

So they were offended at Him, But Jesus said to them, *"A prophet is not without honor except in his own country and in his own house"*.
Matthew 13:57

So when you see the abomination of desolation, spoken by Daniel the **prophet**, standing where it ought not then, then let those who are in Judea flee to the mountains.
Mark 13:14

Nevertheless I must journey today, tomorrow, and the day following: for it cannot be that a **prophet** should perish outside of Jerusalem.
Luke 13:33

And they asked him, "What then? Are you Elijah?" he said, "I am not." "Are you the **prophet?**" And he answered, "No".
John 1:21

Jesus said to her, "Go, call your husband, and come here." The woman answered and said, "I have no husband." Jesus said to her, *"You have well said, "I have no husband.,"* *"for you have had five husbands, and the one whom you now have is not your husband: in that you spoke truly."* The woman said to him, "Sir I perceive that You are a **prophet.**
John 4:16-19

Then those men, when they had seen the sign that Jesus did said, "this is truly the **Prophet** who is to come into the world."
John 6:14

Therefore many from the crowd, when they heard this saying, said, "Truly this is the **Prophet.**"
John 7:40

"King Agrippa, do you believe the **prophets?** I know that you do believe."
Acts 26:27

Having then gifts differing according to the grace that is given to us, let us use them: if prophecy, let us prophesy in proportion to our faith:
Romans 12:6

There are diversities of gifts, but the same Spirit.
I Corinthians 12:4

Now, therefore, you are no longer strangers and foreigners, but fellow citizens with the saints and members of the household of God, having been built on the foundation of the apostles and **prophets**, Jesus Christ Himself being the chief cornerstone.
Ephesians 2:19-20

And he Himself gave some to be apostles, some **prophets**, some evangelists, and some pastors, and teachers, for the **equipping**, of the saints for the work of ministry, for edifying of the body of Christ.
Ephesians 4:11-12

Of this salvation the **prophets** have inquired and searched carefully, who prophesied of the grace that would come to you.
I Peter 1:10

Then he said to me, See that you do not do that, "For I am your fellow servant, and of your brethren the **prophets**, and of those who keep the words of this book. Worship God." And he said to me, Do not seal the words of the prophecy of this book, for the time is at hand.
Revelation 22:9-10

From that time Jesus began to preach and to say, *"Repent, for the kingdom of heaven is at hand."*
Matthew 4:17

As Jesus passed on from there, He saw a man named Matthew sitting at the tax office. And He said to him, *"Follow Me"*. So he arose and followed Him.
Matthew 9:9

Phillip and Bartholomew: Thomas and Matthew the tax collector; James the son of Alphaeus, and Lebbaeus, whose surname was Thaddaeus.
Matthew 10:3

And Jesus came and spoke to them saying, *"All authority has been given to Me in heaven and on earth. Go therefore and make disciples of all the nations, baptizing them in the name of the Fatherand of the Son and of the Holy Spirit, teaching them to observe all things that I have commanded you; and lo, I am with you always, even to the end of the age."* Amen.
Matthew 28:18-20

"But you shall receive power when the Holy Spirit has come upon you; and you shall be witnesses to Me in Jerusalem, and in all Judea and Samaria, and to the end of the earth".
Acts 1:8

Therefore those who were scattered **went everywhere preaching the word**. Then Phillip went down to the city of Samaria and preached Christ to them. And the multitudes with one accord heeded the things spoken by Phillip, hearing and seeing the miracles which he did. For unclean spirits, crying with a loud voice, came out of many who were possessed: and many who were paralyzed and lame were healed. And there was great joy in that city.
Acts 8:4-8

Now when the apostles who were at Jerusalem heard that Samaria had received the word of God, they sent Peter and John to them.
Acts 8:14

Now those who were scattered after the persecution that arose over Stephen traveled as far as Phoenicia, Cyprus, and Antioch, preaching the word to no one but the Jews only. But some of them were men from Cyprus and Cyrene, who, when they had come to Antioch, spoke to the Hellenists, preaching the Lord Jesus. And the hand of the Lord was with them, and a great number believed and turned to the Lord. Then the news of these things came to the ears of the church in Jerusalem, and they sent out Barnabas to go as far as Antioch.
Acts 11:19-22

And Barnabas and Saul returned from Jerusalem when they had **fulfilled their ministry**, and they also took with them John whose surname was Mark.
Acts 12:25

Then Paul, as his custom was, went in to them, and for three Sabbaths reasoned with them from the Scriptures, explaining and demonstrating that the Christ had to **suffer** and rise again from the dead, and saying, **"This Jesus whom I preach to you is the Christ".**
Acts 17:2-3

On the next day we who were Paul's companions departed and came to Caesarea, and entered the house of Phillip the **evangelist**, who was one of the seven, and stayed with him.
Acts 21:8

So, as much as is in me, I am ready to **preach the gospel** to you who are in Rome also.
Romans 1:15

And the Scripture, foreseeing that God would justify the Gentiles by faith, **preached the gospel** to Abraham beforehand, saying, *"In you all the nations shall be blessed."*
Galatians 3:8

That the Gentiles should be fellow heirs, of the same body, and partakers of His promise in Christ through the gospel, of which I became a minister according to the gift of the grace of God given to me by the effective working of His power.
Ephesians 3:6-7

And He himself gave some to be apostles, some prophets, some **evangelists**, and some pastors and teachers, for the **equipping** of the saints for the work of ministry, for the edifying of the body of Christ.
Ephesians 4:11-12

Preach the word! Be ready in season and out of season. Convince, rebuke, exhort, with all longsuffering and teaching. For the time will come when they will not endure sound doctrine, but according to their own desires, because they have itching ears, they will heap up for themselves teachers, and they will turn their ears away from the truth, and be turned aside to fables. But you be watchful in all things, endure afflictions, do the work of an **evangelist**, fulfill your ministry.
II Timothy 4:2-5

Then all the tribes of Israel came to David at Hebron and spoke, saying, "Indeed we are your bone and your flesh. "Also, in time past, when Saul was king over us, you were the one who led Israel out and brought them in; and the Lord said to you, You shall **shepherd** My people Israel, and be ruler over Israel.
II Samuel 5:1-2

And I will give you shepherds according to My heart, who shall feed you knowledge and **understanding**.
Jeremiah 3:15

Indeed they say o me, "Where is the word of the Lord? Let it come now!" As for me, I have not hurried away from being a **shepherd** who follows you. Nor have I desired the woeful day; You know what came out of my lips; It was right there before You.
Jeremiah 17:15-16

"Woe to the **shepherds** who destroy and scatter the sheep of My pasture!" says the LORD. Therefore thus says the LORD God of Israel against the shepherds who feed My people: "You Have scattered My flock, driven them away, and not attended to them. Behold I will attend to you for the evil of your doings," says the LORD.
Jeremiah 23:1-2

My people have been lost sheep, Their **shepherds** have led them astray: They have turned them away on the mountains: They have gone from mountain to hill; They have forgotten their resting place.
Jeremiah 50:6

Son of man prophesy against the **shepherds** of Israel, prophesy and say to them. Thus says the Lord GOD to the shepherds: "Woe to the shepherds of Israel who feed themselves! Should not the shepherds feed the flocks?
Ezekiel 34:2

*"Most assuredly, I say to you, he who does not enter the sheepfold by the door, but climbs up some other way, the same is a thief and a robber. "But he who enters by the door is the **shepherd** of the sheep.*
John 10:1-2

"I am the good shepherd. The good shepherd gives His life for the sheep.
John 10:11

Therefore take heed to yourselves and to all the flock, among which the Holy Spirit has made you overseers, to **shepherd** the church of God which He purchased with His own blood.
Acts 20:28

And He Himself gave some to be apostles, some prophets, some evangelists, and some **pastors** and teachers, for the **equipping** of the saints for the work of ministry, for the edifying of the body of Christ.
Ephesians 4:11-12

If you instruct the brethren in these things, you will be a good minister of Jesus Christ, nourished in the words of faith and of good doctrine which you have carefully followed. Take heed to yourself and to the doctrine. Continue in them, for in doing this you will save both yourself and those who hear you.
I Timothy 4:6, 16

For you were like sheep going astray, but have now returned to the **Shepherd** and Overseer of your souls.
I Peter 2:25

Shepherd the flock of God which is among you, serving as overseers, not by compulsion but willingly, not for dishonest gain but eagerly: nor as being lords over those entrusted to you, but being examples to the flock; and when the Chief **Shepherd** appears, you will receive the crown of glory that does not fade away.
I Peter 5:2-4

So the number of them, with their brethren who were instructed in the songs of the LORD, all who were skillful, was two hundred and eighty eight. And they cast lots for their duty, the small as well as the great, the **teacher** with the student.
I Chronicles 25: 7-8

I have not obeyed the voice of my **teachers**, Nor inclined my ear to those who instructed me!
Proverbs 5:13

And though the Lord gives you, the bread of adversity and the water of affliction, Yet your teachers will not be moved into a corner anymore, but your eyes shall see your **teachers**.
Isaiah 30:20

But you, do not called Rabbi; for One is your Teacher, the Christ, and you are all brethrens.
Matthew 23:8

Now as He was going out on the road, one came running, knelt before Him, and asked Him, "Good **Teacher**, what shall I do that I may inherit eternal life?"
Mark 10:17

This man came to Jesus by night and said to Him, "Rabbi, we know that You are a **teacher** come from God: for no one can do these signs that You do unless God is with him."
John 3:2

You call Me Teacher and Lord; and you say well, for so I am. If I then, your Lord and Teacher, have washed your feet, you also ought to wash one another's feet.
John 13:13-14

Then one in the council stood up, a Pharisee named Gamaliel, a teacher of the law held in respect by all the people, and commanded them to put the apostles outside for a little while.
Acts 5:34

An instructor of the foolish, a **teacher** of babes, having the form of knowledge and truth in the law.
Romans 2:20

And He Himself gave some to be apostles, some prophets, some evangelists, and some pastors and **teachers**, for the **equipping** of the saints for the work of ministry for the edifying of the body of Christ.
Ephesians 4:11-12

From which some, having strayed, have turned aside to idle talk, desiring to be **teachers** of the law, understanding neither what they say not the things which they affirm.
Timothy 1:6-7

For which I was appointed a preacher and an apostle-I am speaking the truth in Christ and not lying-a **teacher** of the Gentiles in faith and truth.
I Timothy 2:7

To which I was appointed a preacher, an apostle, and a **teacher** of the Gentiles.
II Timothy 1:11

Of whom we have much to say, and hard to explain, since you have become dull of hearing. For though by this time you ought to be **teachers**, you need someone to teach you again the first principles of the oracles of God: and you have come to need milk and not solid food. For everyone who partakes only of milk is unskilled in the **word** of righteousness, for he is a babe. But solid food belongs to those who are of full age, that is, those who by reason of use have their senses exercised to **discern both good and evil.**
Hebrews 5:11-14

My brethren, let not many of you become **teachers**, knowing that we shall receive a stricter judgment.
James 3:1

But there were also false prophets among the people, even as there will be false **teachers** among you, who will secretly bring in destructive **heresies**, even denying the Lord who brought them, and bring on themselves swift destruction. And many will follow their destructive ways, because of whom the way of truth will be blasphemed. By covetousness they will exploit you with deceptive words; for long time judgment has not been idle, and their destruction does not slumber.
II Peter 2:1-3

But as for you, speak the things which are proper for sound doctrine: that older men be sober, reverent temperate, sound in faith, in love, in patience: the older women likewise, that they be reverent in behavior, not slanderers, not given to much wine, **teachers** of good things-that they admonish the young women to love their husbands, to love their children.
Titus 2:1-3

All Scriptures from the Spirit Filled Life Bible (NKJV)

Chapter IV Kingdom Carrier

Now Adam knew Eve his wife, and she conceived and born Cain, and said, "I have acquired a man from the LORD." Then she bore again, this time his brother Abel. Now Abel was a keeper of sheep, but Cain was a tiller of the ground.
Genesis 4:1-2

And the Lord visited **Sarah** as He had said, and the LORD did for Sarah as He had spoken. For Sarah conceived and bore Abraham a son in his old age, at the set time of which God had spoken to him. And Abraham called the name of his son who was born to him-whom Sarah bore to him-**Isaac.**
Genesis 21:1-3

Isaac was forty years old when he took **Rebekah** as wife, the daughter of Bethuel the Syrian of Padan Aram, the sister of Laban the Syrian. Now Isaac pleaded with the LORD for his wife, because she was barren; and the Lord granted his plea, and Rebekah his wife conceived. (**Esau and Jacob**)
Genesis 25:20-21; 25-26

Then God remembered **Rachel**, and God listened to her and opened her womb. And she conceived and bore a son, and said, "God has taken away my reproach." So she called his name **Joseph,** and said, "the LORD shall add to me another son."
Genesis 30:22-24

And a man of the house of Levi went and took as **wife** a daughter of Levi. So the woman conceived and bore a son, And when she saw that he was a beautiful child, she hid him three months. And the child grew, and she brought him to Pharaoh's daughter, and he became her son. So she called his name **Moses** saying, "Because I drew him out of the water."
Exodus 2:1-2,10 (read 3-9)

After the death of Moses the servant of the Lord, it came to pass that the Lord spoke to **Joshua** the son of Nun, Moses assistant saying: Moses My servant is dead. Now therefore, arise, go over this Jordan, you and all this people, to the land which I am giving to them-the children of Israel.
Joshua 1:1-2

So Boaz took **Ruth** and she became his wife; and when he went in to her, the LORD gave her conception and she bore a son. Then Naomi took the child and laid him on her bosom, and became a nurse to him. Also the neighbor women gave him a name, saying; "There is a son born to Naomi," And they called his name **Obed**, he is the father of Jesse, the father of David.
Ruth 4:13,16-17

Then they rose early in the morning and worshipped before the LORD, and returned and came to their house at Ramah, And Elkanah knew **Hannah** his wife, and the Lord remembered her. So it came to pass in the process of time that Hannah conceived and bore a son, and called his name **Samuel**, saying, "Because I have asked for him from the LORD."
I Samuel 1:19-20

Thus Jesse made seven of his sons pass before Samuel. And Samuel said to Jesse, "The Lord has not chosen these." And Samuel said to Jesse, "are all the young men here?" Then he said, "There remains yet the youngest, and there he is, keeping the sheep." And Samuel said to Jesse, "Send and bring him. For we will not sit down till he comes here." So he sent and brought him in. Now he was ruddy, with bright eyes, and good-looking, **And the LORD said, "Arise, anoint him: for this is the one!"** Then Samuel took the horn of oil and anointed him in the midst of his brothers; and the Spirit of the LORD came upon **David** from that day forward. So Samuel arose and went to Ramah.
I Samuel 16:10-13

So I came to Jerusalem and was there three days. Then I arose in the night, I and a few men with me; I told no one what my God had put in my heart to do at Jerusalem; nor was there any animal with me, except the one on which I rode. And I went out by night through the Valley gate to the Serpent Well and the Refuse Gate, and viewed the walls of Jerusalem which were broken down and its gates which were burned with fire. (**Nehemiah**)
Nehemiah 2:11-13

And Mordecai had brought up Hadassah, that is, **Esther**, his uncle's daughter for she had neither father nor mother. The young woman was lovely and beautiful. When her father and mother died, Mordecai took her as his own daughter. And it was so, when the king saw Esther the queen standing in the court, that she obtained favor, in his sight; and the king held out to Esther the golden scepter that was in his hand. So Esther drew near, and touched the top of the scepter.
Esther 2:7;5:2

For unto us a Child is born, Unto us a Son is given; And the government will be upon His shoulder. And His name will be called Wonderful, Counselor, Mighty God, Everlasting Father, Prince of Peace. (**Isaiah** the Prophet)
Isaiah 9:6

"Before I formed you in the womb I knew you; Before you were born I sanctified you; I ordained you a prophet to the nations." (**Jeremiah**)
Jeremiah 1:5

Now it came to pass in the thirtieth year, in the fourth month, on the fifth day of the month, as I was among the captives by the River Chebar, that the heavens were opened and I saw visions of God. (**Ezekiel**)
Ezekiel 1:1

But **Daniel** purposed in his **heart** that he would not defile himself with the portion of the king's delicacies, nor with the wine which he drank; therefore he requested of the chief of the eunuchs that he might not defile himself.
Daniel 1:8

Now the birth of **Jesus Christ** was on this wise: When as his mother **Mary** was espoused to Joseph, before they came together, she was found with child of the Holy Ghost. Then Joseph her husband, being a just man, and not willing to make her a public example, was minded to put her away privily. But while he thought of these things, behold, the angel of the Lord appeared unto him in a dream saying, Joseph, thou son of David, fear not to take unto thee **Mary** thy wife; for that which is conceived in her is of the Holy Ghost.
Matthew 1:18-20

Now **Elizabeth's** full time came that she should be delivered: and she brought forth a son. And her neighbors and her cousins heard how the Lord had showed great mercy upon her; and they rejoiced with her. And it came to pass, that on the eight day they came to circumcise the child: and they called him Zacharias, after the name of his father. And his mother answered and said, Not so; but he shall be called **John.**
Luke 1:57-60

And straightway he preached Christ in the synagogues, that he is the Son of God. (**Paul**)
Acts 9:20

And **Peter** said unto him, Aeneas, Jesus Christ maketh thee whole; arise, and make thy bed. And he arose immediately. And all that dwelt at Lydia and Sharon saw him, and turned to the Lord.
Acts 9:34-35

This charge I commit unto thee, son **Timothy,** according to the prophecies which went before on thee, that thou by them mightest war a good warfare: Holding faith, and a good conscience; which some having put away concerning faith have made shipwreck:
I Timothy 1:18-19

To **Titus**, mine own son after the common faith: Grace, mercy, and peace, from God the father and the Lord Jesus Christ our Savior. For this cause left I thee in Crete, that thou shouldest set in order the things that are wanting, and ordain elders in every city, as I had appointed thee.
Titus 1:4-5

James, a servant of God and of the Lord Jesus Christ, to the twelve tribes which are scattered abroad, greeting. My brethren, count it all joy when ye fall into divers temptations: Knowing this, that the trying of your faith worketh patience. But let patience have her perfect work, that ye may be perfect and entire, wanting nothing.
James 1:1-4

Jude, the servant of Jesus Christ, and brother of James to them that are sanctified by God the Father, and preserve in Jesus Christ and called. Mercy unto you, and peace, and love be multiplied. But, beloved , remember ye the words which were spoken before of the apostles of our Lord Jesus Christ: How that they told you there should be mockers in the last time, who should walk after their own ungodly lusts. These be they who separate themselves, sensual, having not the Spirit. But ye, beloved, building up yourselves on your most holy faith, praying in the Holy Ghost.
Jude 1:1-2;17-20

Behold, I come quickly; blessed is he that keepeth the saying of the prophecy of this book. I am Alpha, and Omega, the beginning and the end, the first and the last. I Jesus have sent mine angel to testify unto you these things in the churches. I am the root and the offspring of David, and the bright and morning star. He which testifieth these things saith, *Surely I come quickly.* Amen. Even so, come, Lord Jesus.
(**Jesus** is the Kingdom.)
Revelation 22:7,13,16,20

All Scriptures from the Hebrew-Greek Key Word Study Bible (KJV) and Spirit Filled Life Bible (NKJV)

Chapter V Kingdom Assignment

So God created man in his own image, in the image of God created he him; male and female created he them. And God blessed them, and God said unto them, Be fruitful, and multiply, and replenish the earth, and subdue it: and have dominion over the fish of the sea, and over the fowl of the air, and over every living thing that moveth upon the earth. (Adam and Eve)
Genesis 1:27-28

And God said unto **Noah**, the end of all flesh is come before me; for the earth is filled with violence through them; and, behold, I will destroy them with the earth. **Make thee an ark**, of gopher wood; rooms shalt thou make in the ark, and shalt pitch it within and without with pitch.
Genesis 6:13-14

Now the LORD had said unto **Abram**, Get thee **out** of thy country, and from thy kindred, and from thy father's house, unto a land that I will show thee: And I will make of thee a great nation, and I will bless thee, and make thy name great; and thou shalt be a blessing:
Genesis 12:1-2

And it came to pass after these things, that his master's wife cast her eyes upon **Joseph**; and said, Lie with me. **But he refused,** and said unto his master's wife, Behold, my master wotteth not what is with me in the house, and he hath committed all that he hath to my hand; There is none greater in this house than I; neither hath he kept back any thing from me but thee, because thou art his wife: how then can I do this great wickedness, and **sin against God**. And Joseph was the governor over the land, and he it was that sold to all the people of the land; and Joseph's brethren came, and bowed down themselves before him with their faces to the earth.
Genesis 39:7-9; 42:6

Come now therefore, and I will send thee unto Pharaoh, that thou mayest bring forth my people the children of Israel out of Egypt. And **Moses** said unto God, Who am I, that I should **go** unto Pharaoh, and that I should bring forth the children of Israel out of Egypt? And he said, Certainly I will be with thee: and this *shall* be a token unto thee, that I have sent thee: When thou hast brought forth the people put of Egypt, ye shall serve God upon the mountain.
Exodus 3:10-12

Now after the death of Moses the servant of the LORD it came to pass, that the LORD spake unto **Joshua** the son of Nun, Moses minister saying, Moses my servant is dead; now therefore arise, **go** over this Jordan, thou and all this people, unto the land which I do give to them *even* to the children of Israel. Every place that the sole of your foot shall tread upon, that have I given unto you, as I said unto Moses.
Joshua 1:1-3

And Joshua the son of Nun sent out of Shittim two men to spy secretly, saying, **Go** view the land, even Jericho. And they went, and came into a harlot's house, named **Rahab**, and lodged there. And it was told to the king of Jericho, saying, Behold, there came men in hither tonight of the children of Israel to search out the country. And the king of Jericho sent unto Rahab, saying Bring forth the men that are come to thee, which are entered into thine house: for they be come to search out all the country. And the woman took the two men, and hid them, and said thus, There came men unto me, but I wist not whence they *were*:
Joshua 2:1-4

And the angel of the LORD appeared unto him, and said unto him, The LORD is with thee, thou mighty man of valor, And **Gideon** said unto him, Oh my Lord, if the LORD be with us, why then is all this befallen us? And where be all his miracles which our fathers told us of, saying, Did not the LORD bring us up from Egypt? but now the LORD hath forsaken us, and delivered us into the hands of the Midianites. And the LORD looked upon him, and said, **Go** in this thy might, and thou shalt save Israel from the hand of the Midianites; have not I sent thee?
Judges 6:12-14

And when the words were heard which David spake, they rehearsed them before Saul: and he sent for him. And **David** said to Saul, Let no man's heart fail because of him, they servant will **go** and fight with this Philistine. And Saul said to David, Thou art not able to **go** against this Philistine to fight with him; for thou *art but* a youth and be a man of war from his youth. Thy servant slew both the lion and the bear; and this uncircumcised Philistine shall be as one of them, seeing he hath defiled the armies of the living God.
I Samuel 17:31-36

And **Elijah** the Tishbite, *who was* of the inhabitants of Gilead, said unto Ahab, As the LORD God of Israel liveth, before whom I stand there shall not be dew nor rain these three years, but according to my word. And the word of the LORD came unto him saying, **Get thee hence,** and turn thee eastward, and hide thyself by the brook Cherith, that is before Jordan. And it shall be that thou shalt drink of the brook; and I have commanded the ravens to feed thee there. So he went and did according unto the word of the LORD; for he went and dwelt by the brook Cherith, that is before Jordan.
I Kings 17:1-5

Then the king said unto me, For what dost thou make request? So I prayed to the God of heaven, And I said unto the king, If it please the king, and if thy servant have found favor in thy sight, that thou wouldest **send me** unto Judah, unto the city of my fathers sepulchers, that I may built it. Then I told them of the hand of my God which was good upon me; as also the king's words that

he had spoken unto me. And they said, Let us rise Up and build. So they strengthened their hands for *this* good *work*. (**Nehemiah**)
Nehemiah 2:4-5,18

Then **Esther** bade *them* return Mordecai *this* answer, **Go**, gather together all the Jews that are present in Shushan, and fast ye for me, and neither eat nor drink for **three** days, night or day: I also and my maidens will fast likewise; and so will I **go** in unto the king, which *is* not according to the law: **and if I perish I perish.** So Mordecai went his way, and did according to all that Esther had commanded.

And said, If it please the king, and if I have found favor in his sight, and the thing *seem* right before the king, and I pleasing in his eyes, let it be written to reverse the letters devised by Haman the son of Hammedatha the Agagite, which he wrote to destroy the Jews which are in all the king's provinces. For how can I endure to see the evil that shall come unto my people? Or how can I endure to see the destruction of my kindred? Then the king Ahasuerus said unto Esther the queen and to Mordecai the Jew, Behold, I have given **Esther** the house of Haman, and him they have hanged upon the gallows, because **he laid his hand upon the Jews.**
Esther 4:15-17;8:5-7

There was a man in the land of Uz, whose name *was* Job; and that man was perfect and upright, and one that feared God, and eschewed evil. And the LORD said unto Satan, Whence comest thou? Then Satan answered the LORD, and said, From going to and fro in the earth, and from walking up and down in it. And the LORD said unto **Satan**, Hast thou considered my servant **Job**, that *there is* none like him in the earth, a perfect and an upright man, one that feared God, and escheweth evil? In all this Job sinned not, nor charged God foolishly.
Job 1:1,7-8,22

Except the LORD of hosts had left unto us a very small **remnant**, we should have been as Sodom, *and* we should have been like unto Gomorrah. Hear the word of the LORD, ye rulers of Sodom; give ear unto the law of our God, ye people of Gomorrah. But if ye refuse and rebel, ye shall devoured with the sword: **for the mouth of the LORD hath spoken** *it*. (**Isaiah**)
Isaiah 1:9-10,20

Then the LORD put forth his hand, and touched my mouth, And the LORD said unto me, Behold, **I have put my words in thy mouth.** See, I have this day set thee over the nations and over the kingdoms, to root out, and pull down, and to destroy, and to throw down, to build, and to plant. Thou therefore gird up thy loins, and arise, and **speak unto them all that I command thee**: be not dismayed at their faces, lest I confound thee before them. And they shall fight against thee; but they shall not prevail against thee; for I *am* with thee, saith the LORD to deliver thee. (**Jeremiah**)
Jeremiah 1:9-10,17,19

And he said unto me, Son of man, stand upon thy feet, and **I will speak unto thee.** And the spirit entered into me when he spake unto me, and set me upon my feet, that I heard him that spake unto me. And he said unto me, Son of man, **I send thee** to the children of Israel, to a rebellious nation that hath rebelled against me; they are their fathers have transgressed against me, *even* unto this very day. For they are impudent children and stiffhearted. I do send thee unto them; and thou shalt say unto them, Thus saith the Lord GOD. And they, whether they will hear, or whether they will forbear, (for they *are* a rebellious house,) yet shall know that there hath been a **prophet** among them. (**Ezekiel**)
Ezekiel 2:1-5

Then Daniel **went** in, and desired of the king that he would give him time, and that he would show the king the **interpretation.** Then Daniel went to his house, and made the thing known to Hananiah, Mishael, and Azariah, his companions. That they would desire mercies of the God of heaven concerning this secret; that Daniel and his fellows should not perish with the rest of the wise *men* of Babylon. Then was the secret revealed unto **Daniel** in a night vision. Then Daniel blessed the God of heaven. Daniel answered and said, Blessed be the name of God forever and ever; for **wisdom and might are his;**
Daniel 2:16-19

Then said the LORD unto me, **Go** yet, love a woman beloved of her friend, yet an adulteress, **according to the love of the LORD** toward the children of Israel, who look to other gods, and love flagons of wine. So I bought her to me for fifteen *pieces* of silver, and *for* a homer of barley, and a half homer of barley. And I said unto her, Thou shalt abide for me many days; thou shalt not play the **harlot,** and thou shalt not be for *another* man: so *will* I also *be* for thee. (**Hosea**)
Hosea 3:1-3

The word of the LORD that came to Joel the son of Pethuel. Hear this, ye old men, and give ear, all ye inhabitants of the land. Hath this been in your days, or even in the days of your fathers? Tell ye children of it, and *let* your children *tell* their children, and their children another generation.

Blow ye the trumpet in Zion, and sound an alarm in my holy mountain; let all the inhabitants of the land tremble: **for the day of the LORD cometh, for *it is* nigh at hand.** And it shall come to pass afterward, **that I will pour out my spirit upon all flesh; and your sons and your daughters shall prophesy, your old men shall dream dreams, your young men shall see visions: And also upon the servants and upon the handmaids in those days will I pour out my spirit. And I will show wonders in the heavens and in the earth, blood and fire, and pillars of smoke. The sun shall be turned into darkness, and the moon into blood, before the great and terrible day of the LORD come. And it shall come to pass *that* whosoever shall call on the name of the**

LORD shall be delivered: for in mount Zion and in Jerusalem shall be deliverance, as the LORD hath said, and in the <u>remnant</u> whom the LORD shall call.
(Joel)
Joel 1:1-2;2:1,28-32

Now the word of the LORD came unto **Jonah** the son of Amittai, saying, Arise, **go** to Nineveh, that great city, and cry against it; for their wickedness is come up before me.
Jonah1:1-2

I will stand upon my watch, and set me upon the tower, and will watch to see what he will say unto me, and what I shall answer when I am reproved. And the LORD answered me, and said, **Write the vision, and make *it* plain upon tables, that he may run that readeth it. For the vision is yet for an appointed time,** but at the end it shall speak, and not lie: though it tarry, wait for it: because it will surely come, it will not tarry.
(**Habakkuk**)
Habakkuk 2:1-3

In those days came **John the Baptist,** preaching in the wilderness of Judea. And saying, **Repent ye; for the kingdom of heaven is at hand.** For this is he that was spoken by the prophet Isaiah, saying, The <u>voice</u> of one crying in the wilderness. **Prepare ye the way of the Lord, make his paths straight.** I indeed baptize you with water unto repentance: but he that cometh after me is mightier than I, whose shoe I am not worthy to bear: he shall baptize you **with the Holy Ghost, and with fire**:
Matthew 3:1-3,11

Then was **Jesus led up of the Spirit into the wilderness to be tempted of the devil**. And when he has fasted forty days and forty nights, he was afterward hungry. And when the temper came to him, he said, If thou be the Son of God, command that these stones be made bread. But he answered and said, *It is written, Man shall not live by bread alone, but by every word that proceedeth out of the mouth of God.*
Matthew 4:1-4 (read verses 5:11)

And Jesus, walking by the sea of Galilee, saw two brethren Simon called **Peter,** and **Andrew** his brother, casting a net into the sea for they were fishers. And he saith unto them, *Follow me and I will make you fishers of men.* And they straightway left *their* nets and **followed** him. And going on from thence, he saw other two brethren, **James** the son of Zebedee, and **John** his brother, in a ship with Zebedee their father, mending their nets; and he called them. And they immediately left the ship and their father and **followed** him.
Matthew 4:18-22

And it came to pass in those days, that he went out into a mountain to pray, and continued all night in prayer to God. And when it was day, **he called unto him his disciples: and of them he chose twelve, whom also he named apostles. Simon, (whom he also named Peter,) and Andrew his brother, James and John, Philip and Bartholomew, Matthew and Thomas, James the *son* of Alphaeus, Simon called Zelotes, and Judas *the brother* of James, and Judas Iscariot, which also was the traitor.**
Luke 6:12-16

And they say unto her, Woman, why weepest thou? She saith unto them, because they have taken away my Lord, and I know not where they have laid him. And when she had thus said, she turned herself back, and saw Jesus standing and knew not it was Jesus. Jesus saith unto her, *Woman, why weepest thou? Whom seekest thou?* She, supposing him to be the gardener, saith unto him, Sir, if thou have borne him hence, tell me where Thou hast laid him, and I will take him away. Jesus saith unto her, *Mary,* She turned herself and saith unto him, Rabboni: whixh is to say , Master. Jesus saith unto her, *Touch me not: for I am not yet <u>ascended</u> to my Father: but <u>go</u> to my brethren, and say unto them, I ascend unto my <u>Father</u>, and your Father: and to my God, and your God.* **Mary Magdalene came and told the disciples that she had seen the Lord, and that he had spoken these things unto her.**
John 20:13-18

Therefore let all the houses of Israel know assuredly, that God hath made that same Jesus, whom ye have crucified, both Lord and Christ. Now when they heard *this* they were pricked in their heart, and said unto Peter and to the rest of the apostles, Men and brethren, what shall we do? Then **Peter** said unto them, **Repent, and be baptized every one of you in the name of Jesus Christ for the remission of sins, and ye shall receive the gift of the Holy Ghost.** For the promise is unto you, and to your children, and to all that are afar off, *even* as many as the Lord our God shall call. And with many other words did he testify and exhort saying, Save yourselves from this untoward generation. Then they gladly received his word were baptized: **and the same day there were added *unto them* about three thousand souls.** And they continued steadfastly un the apostles <u>doctrine</u> and <u>fellowship</u>, and in breaking of bread and in <u>prayers.</u>
Acts 2:36-42

And as he journeyed, he came near Damascus: and suddenly there shined round about him a light from heaven: and he fell to the earth, and heard a voice saying unto him, *Saul, why persecuted thou me?* And he said, Who art thou, Lord? And the Lord said, *I am Jesus whom thou persecutest : it is hard for thee to kick against the pricks.* And he trembling and astonished said, Lord, what wilt thou have me to do? And the Lord *said* unto him, *Arise and <u>go</u> into the city, and it shall be told thee what thou must <u>go.</u>* And the Lord *said,* unto him, *Arise, and go into the street which is called Straight, and inquires in the house of Judas for one called Saul of tarsus: for behold, he prayeth, And hath seen in a vision a man named Ananias coming in, and putting his hand on him, that he might receive his sight.*

Then **Ananias** answered, Lord I have heard by many of the man, how much evil he hath done to thy saints at Jerusalem. And here he hath authority from the chief priest to bind all that call on thy name. But the Lord said unto him, *Go thy way: for he is chosen vessel unto me, to bear my name before the Gentiles, and kings, and the children of Israel. For I will show him how great things he must suffer for my name's sake.*
Acts 9:3:-6,11-16

And straightway he <u>preached</u> <u>Christ</u> in the synagogues, that he is the Son of God. But all that heard him, were amazed, and said: Is not this he that destroyed them which called on this name in Jerusalem, and came thither for that intent, that he might bring them bound unto the chief priests? But Saul increased the more in strength, and confounded the Jews which dwelt as Damascus, proving that this is very <u>Christ.</u> **(Paul)**
Acts 9:20-22

This <u>charge</u> I commit unto thee, son **Timothy**, according to the <u>prophecies</u> which went before on thee, that thou by them mightest war a good warfare; Holding faith, and a good conscience; which some having put away concerning faith have made shipwreck: Of whom is Hymenaeus and Alexander; whom I have delivered unto <u>Satan</u>, that they <u>may learn</u> not <u>to blaspheme.</u>
I Timothy 1:18-20

James, a servant of God and of the Lord Jesus Christ, to the twelve tribes which are scattered abroad greeting. Blessed is the man that endureth temptation: for when he is tried, he shall receive the crown of life, which the Lord hath promised to them that love him. Let no man say when he is tempted, I am tempted of God: for god cannot be tempted with evil, neither tempted be any man: but every man is tempted, when he is drawn away of his own lust, and enticed. **Then when lust hath conceived, it bringeth forth sin: and sin, when it is finished, bringeth forth death.** Do not err, my beloved brethren.
James 1:1, 12-16

All Scriptures from the Hebrew-Greek Key Word Study Bible (KJV) and Spirit Filled Life Bible (NKJV)

Chapter VI Kingdom Wealth

But thou shalt remember the LORD thy God: for it is he that giveth thee power to get wealth, that he may establish his covenant which he sware unto thy fathers, as it is this day.
Deuteronomy 8:18

And thou shalt see an <u>enemy</u> *in my* habitation, in all *the wealth* which *God* shall give Israel: and there shall not be an old man in thine house forever.
I Samuel 2:32

And God said to Solomon, Because this was in thine heart, and thou hast not asked riches, wealth, or honor nor the life of thine; enemies, neither yet hast asked long life; but asked wisdom and knowledge for thyself that thou mayest judge my people, over whom I have made king: Wisdom and knowledge is granted unto thee,; **and I will give thee riches, and wealth, and honor, such as none of the kings have had that have been before thee, neither shall there any after thee have the like.**
II Chronicles 1:11-12

For Mordecai the Jew *was* next unto the king Ahasuerus, and great among the Jews, and accepted of the multitude of his brethren, seeking the **wealth** of his people, and speaking peace to all his seed.
Esther 10:3

They spend their days in **wealth**, and in a moment go down to the grave.
Job 21:13

They that trust in their **wealth**, and boast themselves in the multitude of their riches; **None *of them* can by any means redeem his brother, nor give to God a ransom for him**: For the redemption of their soul is precious, and it ceaseth forever. That he should still live forever, and not seek corruption. For he seeth that wise men die, likewise the fool and the brutish person perish, and leave their wealth to others.
Psalm 49:6-10

Wealth and riches shall be in his house: and his righteousness endureth forever.
Psalm 112:3

The rich man's **wealth** *is* his strong city: the destruction of the poor *is* their poverty.
Proverbs 10:15

Wealth *gotten* by vanity shall be diminishes: but he that gathereth by labor shall increase.
Proverbs 13:11

The rich man's **wealth** *is* his strong city, and as a high wall in his own conceit.
Proverbs 18:11

Whom he called together with the workmen of like occupation, and said, Sirs, ye know that by this craft we have our **wealth**.
Acts 19:25

Let no man seek his own, but every man another's ***wealth.***
I Corinthians 10:24

For wisdom is a defense, and **money** is a defense: but the excellency of knowledge is, that wisdom giveth life to them that have it.
Ecclesiastes 7:12

Shake thyself from the dust; arise, and sit down, O Jerusalem: loose thyself from the bands of thy neck, O captive daughter of Zion. For thus <u>saith</u> the LORD, Ye have sold yourselves for naught; and ye <u>shall be redeemed</u> without **money.**
Isaiah 52:2-3

Wherefore do ye spend **money** for *that which is* not bread? And your labor for *that which* satisfieth not? <u>hearken</u> diligently unto me, and eat ye that which is good, and let your soul delight itself in fatness.
Isaiah 55:2

But he that had received one went and digged in the earth, and hid his lord's money.
Matthew 25:18

But Peter said unto him, Thy **money** perish with thee, because thou hast thought that the gift of God may be purchased with money.
Acts 8:20

For the love of money is the root of all evil: which while some coveted after, they have the erred from the faith, and pierced themselves through with many sorrows.
I Timothy 6:10

All Scriptures from the Hebrew-Greek Key Word Study Bible (KJV)